BBC

GCSE BITESIZE revision

Maths

Intermediate Level

Graham Lawlor

Consultant: Rob Kearsley Bullen

Published by BBC Worldwide Limited,
Woodlands, 80 Wood Lane, London W12 0TT

First published 2002

Reprinted 2002, 2003, June 2004

ISBN: 0 563 50130 8

Colour reproduction by Tien Wah Press Pte Ltd, Singapore
Printed and bound by Tien Wah Press Pte Ltd, Singapore

Acknowledgements
Illustrations by Hardlines Ltd.

BBC

Contents

Data handling

Exam questions and model answers

Topic checker

Complete the facts

Answers to practice questions

Answers to check questions

Glossary

Last-minute learner

Introduction

About Bitesize

GCSE Bitesize is a revision service designed to help you achieve success at GCSE. There are books, television programmes and a website, each of which provides a separate resource designed to help you get the best results.

The television programmes are available on video through your school or you can find out transmission times by calling **08700 100 222**.

The website can be found at
http://www.bbc.co.uk/schools/gcsebitesize/maths

About this book

This book is your all-in-one revision companion for GCSE.
It gives you the three things you need for successful revision:

1 every topic, clearly organised and clearly explained
2 the most important facts and ideas highlighted for quick checking
3 all the practice you need – in the check questions in the margins, in the practice section at the end of each topic, and in the exam questions section at the end of this book.

Each topic is organised in the same way:

■ **The bare bones** – a summary of the main points, an introduction to the topic, and a good way to check what you know

■ **Key facts** highlighted throughout

■ **Check questions** in the margin at the end of each section of the topic - have you understood this bit?

■ **Remember tips** in the margin – extra advice on this section of the topic

■ **Exam tips** in red – specific things to bear in mind for the exam

■ **Practice questions** at the end of each topic – a range of questions to check your understanding.

The extra sections at the back of this book will help you check your progress and be confident that you know your stuff. They include:

■ a selection of **Exam questions and model answers** explained to help you get full marks, plus extra questions for you to try for yourself, with answers

■ a **Topic checker** with quick questions in all topic areas

■ a **Complete the facts** section

■ a **Last-minute learner** – the most important facts in just four pages.

About the GCSE maths exam

Your school or college is in communication with an examination board, such as AQA, EdExcel or OCR, and will enter you officially for the maths exam. If you want more information about what you need to know, the specification of your exam can be downloaded from their websites.

The exam usually consists of three parts:

- Paper 1 covers Number and Algebra, Shape, Space and Measures, and Data Handling. You are not allowed to use a calculator on this paper.

- Paper 2 covers the same topics as Paper 1. A calculator is essential on this paper.

- Coursework assignments covering Using and Applying Mathematics, or a third examination paper designed to test this area.

Preparing for the exam

Check your equipment about a week before the exam. Make sure you have a couple of decent pens, at least two sharpened pencils or a refill for your mechanical pencil, a set of mathematical instruments (ruler, protractor, compass), your calculator and a transparent container for all of it (a sandwich bag is OK).

Check the condition of your calculator's batteries. If in any doubt, replace them with a new set about two days before Paper 2, as you will need your calculator for this paper. Make sure it is working properly – that way, you've got time to go out and replace them again if they're duff!

Maths exams tend to be in the morning. This is good, because you are usually sharper then than in the afternoon. You can take advantage of this by getting up extra early on the day of the exam, if you want to, and doing a bit of cramming using the Last-minute learner on page 125 of this book. Have a good breakfast so you have plenty of energy, and make sure you bring a drink with you.

If the weather's really hot, exam halls can be very unpleasant to sit in. Dress appropriately: some schools insist on uniform, others don't, but you can usually compensate for the weather in some way!

In the exam room

When you are issued with your exam paper, you must not open it immediately. However, there are some details on the front cover that you can fill in (your name, centre number, etc.) before you start the exam itself. If you're not sure where to write these details, ask one of the invigilators (teachers supervising the exam).

You are expected to write your answers in the exam booklet provided. This means that co-ordinate grids, triangular dotted paper, etc. are all printed for you, so you don't need to use extra paper.

During the exam

When you open your exam paper, have a look through it (all the way through). Make sure that all the pages are there.

Note how many questions there are. That will give you an idea how long you can afford to spend on each question.

How the exams are marked

Most questions have a combination of method marks and answer marks. It should be obvious what these mean:

■ **method marks** are awarded for correct working or approach

■ **answer marks** are awarded for the right thing appearing in the answer space.

When questions have more than one part, you often have to carry an answer through from one part to the next. If you make a mistake, you will be penalised for that, but only once. In most cases, the examiners have instructions to follow-through your mistake and see if you've worked correctly from that point on. More work for them, but fair on you!

Organising your revision

Studying maths is different to studying other subjects, because the only way to learn maths is to do maths. Simply reading through your notes is not enough in maths, you do have to put in the time and effort and actually tackle the questions.

The best way to study is to take an hour-long session, split it into three fifteen-minute sessions and have three five-minute breaks. Don't save all the breaks up to the end – you won't learn as effectively. You need to make sure that you split your sessions up in this way, it really does improve your learning. Taking breaks in this way allows your brain time to sort out the information.

Techniques to help you remember

There are things that you can do to enhance your memory as you revise.

■ **Shapes** – Imagine that you had to remember five different types of numbers, for example: primes, squares, cubes, triangular numbers, and the Fibonacci sequence.

One easy way to remember these five facts is to draw them around a pentagon:

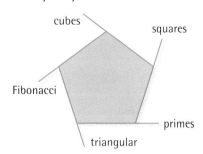

You can then add diagrams onto the pentagon. The act of actually drawing the pentagon and labelling it makes it a worthwhile learning activity. It gives you a hook to remember. The fact that the pentagon has five sides means that you know you have to remember five facts. This can work in any subject.

Imagine you had five categories of information to memorise and each category had three smaller sets of facts. You could develop your shape memory-jogger to look like the one we've drawn on the left.

Here, the five facts can be listed around the pentagon and each subsection of three facts can be listed around each small triangle.

If some of the sub-sections have only one fact, instead of using a triangle, use a circle. The shape memory-jogger is fun, creative and uses both sides of your brain.

- **Chunking** – This means grouping facts together. For instance, one of the easiest ways to remember phone numbers is to group the digits in threes. So if you can group material, it will make it easier to remember.

- **Images** – Making images is creative, involving you more actively in the process of revising, helping you to remember. In your revision notes, make pictures and images as often as you can. Good images:
    - are colourful
    - are lively and dynamic
    - can make you laugh
    - often have exaggerated aspects to them.

Author's note

Being the author of this book simply means I am part of a team. Therefore, I need to put on record my thanks to Nick Jones and the team at the BBC for their faith in me, in particular Sarah Jenkin and Kate Sleigh, Rob Kearsley Bullen, and also my colleague Jane Furlong of Soar Valley College in Leicester for her invaluable advice.

Finally my thanks to my partner Judith Lawlor for her support during the writing of this book, without which I could never have completed the task.

Money, time and distance

THE BARE BONES

➤ The four basic rules of number are addition, subtraction, multiplication and division.

➤ Addition and subtraction are inverse (opposites) – they undo each other.

➤ Multiplication and division are inverses too – they undo each other.

A Money

1 A meal in a restaurant costs £9.70 per person.
How many people were in a group who paid £48.50 in total?

2 Look carefully at the question. What are you being asked to do?
You are being asked to find out how many people were in the group.

3 First write down what you know:
total amount spent = £48.50   cost per person = £9.70

4 Now decide what maths you need to use. You need to divide:
£48.50 ÷ £9.70 = 5

5 The number of people in the group is 5.

6
> Money questions can include conversions between currencies, percentage increases and decreases, and dividing sums in a ratio.

Q How could you check your answer?

KEY FACT

> In an exam, you often have to take the question apart and decide what kind of maths you need.

B Time

1 My grandfather died in the year 2002 at the age of 93 and left me his clock in his will. The clock was made 15 years before he was born.

When was my grandfather born?

When was the clock made?

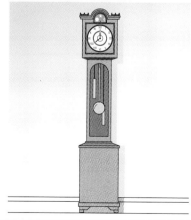

2 Write down what you know:
He died in 2002 and he was 93 when he died.

3 Use subtraction to find the date he was born:
2002 − 93 = 1909

4 The clock was made 15 years before he was born. So use subtraction again:

1909 − 15 = 1894

5 The clock was built in 1894.

6 Questions on time can involve evaluating time intervals (e.g. length of a television programme), graphs of journeys, speed and distance.

Q In what century does 1894 lie?

KEY FACT

1 century = 100 years

C Distance

1 This table gives distances in miles between some cities in the UK. The same cities are listed across the top and down the side.

	Bristol	Cambridge	Cardiff	Edinburgh	Liverpool	York
Bristol		148	45	379	183	227
Cambridge	148		179	334	186	154
Cardiff	45	179		394	198	243
Edinburgh	379	334	394		221	199
Liverpool	183	186	198	221		100
York	227	154	243	199	100	

KEY FACT

To find the distance between two places, find your starting point along the top row. Find your destination on the left-hand side. Read down the column from the top and along the row from the side, until you find the box where they meet.

Q Explain why some of the boxes in the table above are blanked out.

2 Example: A group of tourists are planning a trip around the UK. Starting at Edinburgh, they want to travel no more than 200 miles in one day. On the second day, they want to visit Cambridge and then stay in Bristol. Where would you recommend that they stop for the night?

From Edinburgh, you can recommend York, 199 miles away. This is the only city less than 200 miles away.

How far will they travel during the second day?

York to Cambridge = 154 miles
Cambridge to Bristol = 148 miles
Total = 302 miles

PRACTICE

1 There are 472 students in a college. There are 152 female students. How many male students attend the college?

2 Find two numbers that add up to 13 but multiply to equal 36.

3 How much is 12 litres of paint, if one litre costs £3.40?

4 I spend £14.20 in a shop and give the sales assistant a £20 note. How much change will I get?

5 Which four coins make a total of £1.27?

6 A bus leaves Betws-yn-Rhos at 15:30 and will get to Llandudno Junction in 45 minutes. What time will the bus arrive at Llandudno Junction?

7 A clock stopped at 07:15 on Thursday and was restarted at 13:20 on Friday. How long did the clock stop for?

Working with fractions

THE BARE BONES

➤ The top of a fraction is called the numerator and the bottom is called the denominator.

➤ Fractions that contain different numbers but mean the same thing are equivalent. Given a fraction, the numerators and denominators of its equivalent fractions make simple sequences of multiples.

➤ The equivalent fraction with the smallest numbers is in 'lowest terms'.

A Equivalent fractions

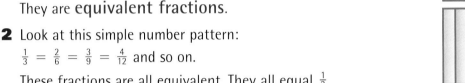

1 This diagram shows that $\frac{1}{3}$ is the same as $\frac{2}{6}$. It covers the same fraction of the diagram.

They are **equivalent fractions**.

2 Look at this simple number pattern:

$\frac{1}{3} = \frac{2}{6} = \frac{3}{9} = \frac{4}{12}$ and so on.

These fractions are all equivalent. They all equal $\frac{1}{3}$.

3 The fractions equivalent to $\frac{1}{3}$ contain numbers that make sequences.

$$\frac{1}{3} = \frac{1 \times 2}{3 \times 2} = \frac{1 \times 3}{3 \times 3} = \frac{1 \times 4}{3 \times 4}, \text{etc.}$$

Q Write down five fractions equivalent to $\frac{3}{4}$.

B Improper fractions and mixed numbers

Improper fractions are top-heavy fractions. In other words they are fractions where the <u>numerator is larger than the denominator</u>, e.g. $\frac{5}{4}$.

Mixed numbers are whole numbers and fractions, eg $1\frac{1}{2}$.

1 Changing improper fractions to mixed numbers.

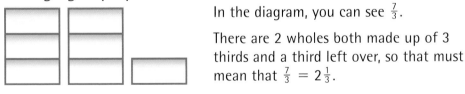

In the diagram, you can see $\frac{7}{3}$.

There are 2 wholes both made up of 3 thirds and a third left over, so that must mean that $\frac{7}{3} = 2\frac{1}{3}$.

Remember
On your calculator, look for the $a\frac{b}{c}$ button. This is your fraction button.

2 Changing mixed numbers into improper fractions.

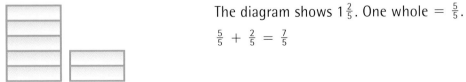

The diagram shows $1\frac{2}{5}$. One whole $= \frac{5}{5}$.

$$\frac{5}{5} + \frac{2}{5} = \frac{7}{5}$$

The fraction part of the number is in fifths, so you need to convert it all to fifths.

From the diagram, you can see that the whole block is split into $\frac{5}{5}$ and there are $\frac{2}{5}$ left over, so the answer is $\frac{7}{5}$.

Q Key in:
1 $a\frac{b}{c}$ 3 on your calculator.
What fraction do you get?

C   Adding and subtracting fractions

Remember
Only add or subtract the numerators of fractions when the denominators are the same.

1 $\frac{1}{2} + \frac{1}{3} = ?$ You can see in this sum that the fractions have different denominators. You need to make both denominators the same before you can add them.

2 $\frac{1}{2} = \frac{2}{4} = \left(\frac{3}{6}\right) = \frac{4}{8} = \frac{5}{10}$

$\frac{1}{3} = \left(\frac{2}{6}\right) = \frac{3}{9} = \frac{4}{12} = \frac{5}{15}$

The lowest denominator that is in both lists is 6.

> Given any two fractions, you can always find pairs of fractions with the same denominator that are equivalent to them. One of these pairs has the smallest denominator. This number is the <u>lowest common denominator (LCD)</u> of the two original fractions.

KEY FACT

3 Here we have changed them both to sixths: $\frac{1}{2} = \frac{3}{6}$ and $\frac{1}{3} = \frac{2}{6}$.

4 So $\frac{1}{2} + \frac{1}{3} = ?$ can be written as: $\frac{3}{6} + \frac{2}{6} = \frac{5}{6}$.

5 Subtraction works in the same way.

What is $\frac{5}{8} - \frac{7}{12}$?

Q Can you work out $\frac{1}{3} + \frac{1}{4}$ using this method?

The LCD for eighths and twelfths is 24, so change both fractions to 24ths.

$\frac{5}{8} = \frac{15}{24}$ and $\frac{7}{12} = \frac{14}{24}$.

$\frac{5}{8} - \frac{7}{12} = \frac{15}{24} - \frac{14}{24} = \frac{1}{24}$.

D   Multiplying and dividing fractions

1 To multiply two fractions together, simply multiply top by top and bottom by bottom.

$\frac{5}{8} \times \frac{4}{15} = \frac{5 \times 4}{8 \times 15} = \frac{20}{120}$. This cancels to $\frac{1}{6}$.

You can always get the answer this way, but it can sometimes lead to a lot of cancelling.

2 It can be easier to cross-cancel. This means doing some of the cancelling before you multiply.

3 Mixed numbers must be converted to improper fractions first.

To divide two fractions, invert the second one (turn it upside down) and turn the ÷ into a ×.

Q What is $\frac{3}{4} \times 5\frac{1}{3}$?

PRACTICE

1 Work out the equivalent fractions:

   (a) $\frac{1}{2} = \frac{}{6}$ (b) $\frac{3}{4} = \frac{9}{}$

2 Change these improper fractions to mixed numbers:

   (a) $\frac{15}{4}$ (b) $\frac{22}{7}$ (c) $\frac{51}{5}$ (d) $\frac{82}{9}$

3 Change these mixed numbers to improper fractions:

   (a) $4\frac{1}{3}$ (b) $12\frac{1}{8}$ (c) $9\frac{7}{9}$ (d) $27\frac{3}{4}$

Working with indices

THE BARE BONES

➤ Powers are made up of a base and an index. In 12^5, 12 is the base and 5 is the index. 12^5 means $12 \times 12 \times 12 \times 12 \times 12$.

➤ Powers of the same base can be multiplied/divided easily by adding/subtracting indices.

➤ Negative indices are reciprocals and fractional indices are roots.

A Multiplying and dividing indices

1 Rule for multiplying
Add the indices when the bases are the same.

$$\text{base} \rightarrow a^{\,m} \leftarrow index$$

KEY FACT

In algebra, the rule for multiplying indices is $a^m \times a^n = a^{m+n}$

Remember
You can only do this if the bases are the same.

In the sum $4^2 \times 4^3$, the bases are the same (4).
So to multiply, you have to add the indices: $4^2 \times 4^3 = 4^{(2+3)} = 4^5$

2 Rule for dividing
Subtract the indices when the bases are the same.

KEY FACT

In algebra, the rule for dividing indices is $a^m \div a^n = a^{m-n}$

In the sum $5^6 \div 5^2$, the bases are the same (5).

So to divide, you have to subtract the indices:

$5^6 \div 5^2 = 5^{(6-2)} = 5^4$

Q Use this method to work out:
(a) $2^2 \times 2^7$
(b) $7^7 \div 7^2$

B How to deal with powers raised to powers

1 Look at this calculation:

$(4^3)^2 = (4 \times 4 \times 4) \times (4 \times 4 \times 4)$

$= 4 \times 4 \times 4 \times 4 \times 4 \times 4$

$= 4^6$

Remember
Any number to the power 1 is just the number:
$5^1 = 5$.

To raise a power to a power, <u>multiply the indices</u> together.
In algebra, $(a^m)^n = a^{m \times n}$

KEY FACT

2 So, this means that:

$(4^3)^2 = 4^6$

Q Can you show how to generate 4^9 from 4^3?

C How to deal with negative powers

1 When you use the index rule for division, you can end up with a **negative index**. For example, $3^2 \div 3^5 = 3^{2-5}$
$$= 3^{-3}$$

2 You can write it in a different way:
$$\frac{3^2}{3^5} = \frac{\cancel{3} \times \cancel{3}}{\cancel{3} \times \cancel{3} \times 3 \times 3 \times 3} = \frac{1}{3 \times 3 \times 3} = \frac{1}{3^3}$$

3 So $3^{-3} = \frac{1}{3^3} = \frac{1}{3 \times 3 \times 3} = \frac{1}{27}$.

4 In general, $a^{-n} = \frac{1}{a^n}$.

5 When two numbers are multiplied together and the answer is 1, the numbers are said to be **reciprocals** of each other. So the reciprocal of 4 is $\frac{1}{4}$ because when they are multiplied, the **answer is 1**.

 Can you write 2^{-5} as a fraction?

D How to deal with fractional indices

1 Fractional indices mean **roots**.

2 You should know that $\sqrt{16} = 4$

3 The rule of indices tells you that 16 is 16^1. If you use this rule, then $\sqrt{16} \times \sqrt{16} = 16$ (and 4×4 does equal 16).

4 $\sqrt{16}$ must be the same as $16^{\frac{1}{2}}$.
This makes sense because $16^{\frac{1}{2}} \times 16^{\frac{1}{2}} = 16^1$ ($\frac{1}{2} + \frac{1}{2} = 1$).

5 The same argument applies to $\sqrt[3]{a}$. This can be written as $a^{\frac{1}{3}}$.

Q Can you rewrite $x^{\frac{1}{4}}$?

EY FACT

In general: $\sqrt[n]{a} = a^{\frac{1}{n}}$

 PRACTICE

1 Work out:
(a) $9^{\frac{1}{2}}$ (b) $9^{-\frac{1}{2}}$ (c) $9^{\frac{3}{2}}$

2 Work out the following, writing your answers in both index form and without using indices where possible.
(a) 14^0 (b) $(5^2)^{-3}$ (c) $36^{\frac{1}{2}}$ (d) $64^{-\frac{1}{2}}$

3 Work out $16^{\frac{1}{2}} \times 8^{\frac{1}{3}}$.

4 What is $49^{\frac{1}{2}} \times 49^{\frac{1}{2}}$?

5 Calculate $64^{\frac{1}{2}} \div 2^3$.

Numbers in standard form

THE BARE BONES
- In science, you often need to use very large or very small numbers.
- 6.1×10^5, 9×10^{-3} and 8.01×10^{12} are examples of numbers in standard form.
- Numbers not in index form are in 'ordinary' form.

A What is standard form?

KEY FACT

In standard form, large or small numbers are written in the form $a \times 10^n$, where $1 \leq a < 10$ and n is a positive or negative integer.

Remember
$10^1 = 1$
$10^2 = 100$
$10^3 = 1000$
$10^6 = 1\,000\,000$

Q Why are they not in standard form?

1 So these numbers **are** in standard form:
1.5×10^6 2.848×10^{-4} 8×10^{11}.
but these are not:
62×10^3 2100×10^5 0.06×10^{-3}.

2 The numbers above are in index form, but not in standard index form

B Writing large numbers in standard form

1 To write a number in standard form:
- write it as a decimal multiplied by a power of ten (10, 1 000 000 etc.)
- write the power of ten using an index (10^2, 10^6 etc.).

2 Write 3000 in standard form: $3000 = 3 \times 1000$
$= 3 \times 10^3$.

3 Write 240 in standard form: $240 = 2.4 \times 100$
$= 2.4 \times 10^2$.

4 Write 388 000 000 in standard form:
$388\,000\,000 = 3.88 \times 100\,000\,000 = 3.88 \times 10^8$.

Q In the last example, the number has 6 zeros. Why isn't the index number 6?

C Numbers less than 1

Remember

$10^{-1} = 0.1$

$10^{-2} = 0.01$

$10^{-3} = 0.001$

$10^{-6} = 0.000\ 001$

1 Numbers less than 1 have a <u>negative index</u> when written in standard form.

2 Write 0.0007 in standard form.

In this example, 0.0007 is written as $7 \times \frac{1}{10\ 000}$. 10 000 would be written as 10^4 in standard form, but it has been written as $\frac{1}{10\ 000}$, which is $\frac{1}{10^4} = 10^{-4}$.

So, $0.0007 = \frac{1}{10\ 000}$

$\qquad = 7 \times \frac{1}{10^4}$

$\qquad = 7 \times 10^{-4}$.

Q Is there a connection between the number of zeros after the decimal point and the index?

3 Write 0.0224 in standard form.

$0.0224 = 2.24 \times \frac{1}{100}$

$\qquad = 2.24 \times 10^{-2}$.

C Changing standard form to ordinary form

1 To change a standard form number to ordinary form:

- write it as a decimal multiplied by a power of ten (1000, $\frac{1}{100}$ etc.)

- multiply the decimal by the power.

2 Change 3.4×10^4 to ordinary form.

$3.4 \times 10^4 = 3.4 \times 10\ 000$

$\qquad = 34\ 000$

Q What is number 2×10^{12} in ordinary form? How would you pronounce it?

3 Write 6.88×10^{-6} without indices.

$6.88 \times 10^{-6} = 6.88 \times \frac{1}{1\ 000\ 000}$

$\qquad = 0.000\ 006\ 88$.

PRACTICE

1 Write in standard form:

(a) 600   (b) 2 000 000   (c) 41 000   (d) 955 000

(e) 0.0009   (f) 0.003   (g) 0.00000101   (h) 0.58.

2 Write in ordinary form:

(a) 8×10^3 (b) 4×10^5 (c) 2.1×10^9 (d) 7.003×10^7

(e) 3×10^{-1} (f) 5×10^{-8} (g) 5.75×10^{-2} (h) 6.77×10^{-6}.

THE BARE BONES

➤ Calculations using standard form numbers may be done manually in simple cases.

➤ Scientific calculators accept and display numbers in standard form.

A Manual calculations

1 To multiply two standard form numbers, rearrange the calculation to bring the index parts of the numbers together. These can be multiplied using the index laws (see page 12).
You may need to adjust the answer slightly to bring it into standard form.

KEY FACT ▶ Standard form numbers in calculations are often enclosed in brackets. This is usually just to make them easier to read.

- What is $(3 \times 10^4) \times (7 \times 10^3)$?

$$(3 \times 10^4) \times (7 \times 10^3) = (3 \times 7) \times (10^4 \times 10^3) \quad \textit{rearrange the calculation}$$
$$= 21 \times 10^7 \qquad \textit{multiply numbers and add indices}$$
$$= 2.1 \times 10^8 \qquad \textit{convert to standard form.}$$

2 When adding or subtracting, you may need to change one of the numbers so it's no longer in standard form. The indices in the two numbers have to match.

- What is $(2.1 \times 10^{11}) + (1.6 \times 10^{12})$?

It makes most sense to change the smaller number to match the larger one.

$$(2.1 \times 10^{11}) + (1.6 \times 10^{12}) = (0.21 \times 10^{12}) + (1.6 \times 10^{12}) \qquad \textit{change small number}$$
$$= 1.81 \times 10^{12} \textit{ add the numbers – the index remains the same}$$

Q Have a go at $(1.06 \times 10^9) - (9 \times 10^7)$ this way.

B On a calculator – the EXP button

Remember
The standard form key on your calculator may be labelled: EXP, EE, E or $\times 10^x$.

1 On your calculator you have a button like this EXP , for entering numbers in standard form.

2 If you key in [4] [.] [5] [EXP] [7] , you should get $\boxed{45000000}$ on your display. You have entered 4.5×10^7 into your calculator.

3 To key a number with a negative index, follow your calculator's instructions for negative numbers. On older calculators, to enter 7.3×10^{-8}, you might need to key in [7] [.] [3] [EXP] [8] [+/−].

On a modern direct logic calculator, it's more likely to be:
[7] [.] [3] [EXP] [(−)] [8].

Q Enter 2×10^{-3} into your calculator. Then press [=] . What does the display show?

C How your calculator displays standard form

1 Enter a standard form number with a large index into your calculator and press $=$.

If you've entered a number that's too big for the standard display, you will have activated the standard form display mode. For example, if you've entered 1.5×10^{14}, the display could look like one of these:

| 1.5^{14} |

2 Once you're familiar with this display mode, try entering a standard form number with a large negative index (e.g. 6.25×10^{-10}). The display should follow the same pattern as before, but the minus sign in the index should be clearly visible.

3 Most calculators can display numbers with a maximum index of 99. A result larger than this will give an error.

Q Find a calculation, not using standard form numbers, that causes a display error because the answer is too big.

D Doing calculations

1 There is no difference between doing calculations with ordinary form numbers and standard from numbers. You can also mix them up in the same calculation. Just follow the usual rules:

- Enter the first number and operation $(+, -, \times, \div, x^y, \sqrt{\ }$ etc.), in the right order.
- If necessary, enter the second number and press $=$.

KEY FACT

When you use standard form numbers in a calculation, the answer may be within the calculator's normal display range, and be displayed without an index, so you may have to convert it yourself.

2 Calculate: $(8 \times 10^3) \times (4 \times 10^3)$. Key in:

| 8 | EXP | 3 | × | 4 | EXP | 3 |

to get 3.2×10^7.

3 Calculate: $(5 \times 10^8)^2$.

Key in: | 5 | EXP | 8 | x^2 | to get 2.5×10^{17}.

Q What types of calculation don't need a second number?

PRACTICE

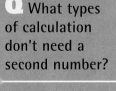

1 Calculate 5^{75}. Give your answer in standard form, correct to 3 s.f.

2 If $x = 2 \times 10^{12}$ and $y = 3 \times 10^5$
find (a) xy (b) $\frac{x}{y}$.

3 Work out $(3.1 \times 10^{-4}) \times (4.3 \times 10^{12})$.

4 Work out $(3.7 \times 10^{-6})^2$.

5 Given that $M = \sqrt{\frac{n}{p}}$, find M in standard form when $n = 3.6 \times 10^2$ and $p = 1.6 \times 10^4$.

Sequences

➤ A sequence is a set of numbers that are connected in some way.
➤ Multiples are the results of multiplying a particular number by another positive whole number, so the multiples of 6 are 6, 12, 18, 24 etc.
➤ The factors of a number are the whole numbers that divide exactly into that number, so the factors of 4 are 1, 2 and 4. (The number itself and one are also factors of a number.)

A Finding prime factors using a ladder

Remember
A prime number is a number greater than 1, which has only two factors.

Q Use this method to find the prime factors of 100.

To write a number as a product of its prime factors, you can draw a division ladder like this, putting the target number, let's say 30, at the top on the right.

2	30
3	15
5	5
	1

Choose the first prime number that is a factor of 30, in this case 2, and put it in the left column.

Divide the target number, 30, by the prime factor, 2. Put the answer below the 30.

Repeat this if possible. So will 2 go into 15? No, so pick the next prime factor, which is 3. Will 3 divide into 15? Yes.

Continue until you have 1 in the base of the right-hand side of the ladder.

Read down the left-hand column. This is the list of prime factors. So $30 = 2 \times 3 \times 5$.

B Squares and cubes

Make sure you are familiar with these sequences. They regularly turn up on exam papers and mean easy marks.

Remember
Squared means multiplied by itself.

KEY FACT

Q Write down all of the squares and cubes up to 200.

KEY FACT

1 Look at this pattern:

1 4 9 16 25 36 49

What is the same about all of these numbers?
The sequence is built up by 1×1, then 2×2, then 3×3 and so on. These are called **square numbers**.

Square numbers form square patterns.

1   4   9   16

2 Cube numbers are built up in a similar way, the sequence is 1, 8, 27 etc and is built up from $1 \times 1 \times 1$, $2 \times 2 \times 2$, then $3 \times 3 \times 3$ and so on.

Cube numbers have 3 parts, like the 3 dimensions in a cube.

27 is a cube number because it is $3 \times 3 \times 3$.

C Triangular numbers

1 Look at the shape of this pattern:

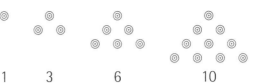

1   3   6   10

> The numbers can be arranged as triangles so they are called 'triangular numbers'.

2 Look at how the pattern builds up. The first number is 1, the second number is 2 + 1 (3), the third number is 3 + 2 + 1 (6), so the fourth must be 4 + 3 + 2 + 1 and so on. The nth triangular number is $\frac{n(n+1)}{2}$.

Q What is the next number in the sequence?

D The Fibonacci sequence

1 Look at this pattern:

1	1	2	3	5	8	13	21	34 . . .

2 It is a famous sequence discovered by a medieval Italian mathematician called Fibonacci.

3 The Fibonacci sequence uses **subsequent addition**, in other words 1 + 1, then 1 + 2, then 2 + 3, then 3 + 5 and so on.

Q Can you see how this sequence is building up?

E Perfect numbers

1 Work out the factors of 6. They are 1, 2, 3 and 6. Now add all of the factors except 6: 1 + 2 + 3
Compare your answer with the number you started with (6). What do you notice?

2 6 is called a perfect number, for this reason.

Q What is the next perfect number?

PRACTICE

1 Find the factors of: (a)   40   (b)   100   (c)   85.

2 Express these numbers as a product of their prime factors:
(a)   360   (b)   22   (c)   90.

3 What are the prime numbers between 30 and 50?

4 What are the square numbers between 100 and 150?

5 What are the next two cube numbers after 27?

6 List the triangular numbers between 6 and 30.

7 Write down the multiples of 5 less than 50, which are also multiples of 4.

8 What factors of 100 are also multiples of 4?

9 What multiples of 5 less than 100 are also multiples of 6?

Ratio, proportion and percentages

➤ Ratios give us a way of comparing quantities.

➤ Proportion shows us that as one quantity increases or decreases, a corresponding quantity does the same.

➤ Percentages are commonly used to determine increases and decreases.

A Ratio

KEY FACT

> The ratio of one quantity to another is written as $a:b$ or $\frac{a}{b}$.

1 Maps are drawn to scale. A common scale is 2 cm to 1 km. This means that 2 cm on the map stands for a real distance of 1 km. Another way of saying this is 1 : 50 000. This is a ratio.

> Be careful! The order in which the comparison is made has to be clear. $a:b$ is not equal to $b:a$.

2 The two quantities must be in the same units and the answer must be in the simplest form. **Simplest form means it cannot be cancelled further.**

KEY FACT

> <u>Unitary ratios</u> are ratios that can be written in the form <u>1:n</u> or n : 1. The number n is either a decimal or a whole number.

3 Express this ratio in the simplest form – a length of 36 m to 48 m.

First find the **highest common factor** of 36 and 48. This is 12. Now divide by it. This means 36 : 48 cancels to 3 : 4.

4 Increase £4.50 in the ratio 3 : 2. Call the new amount £x; then £x : £4.50 = 3 : 2. Write this as a fraction: $\frac{x}{4.50} = \frac{3}{2}$.

$$2x = £13.50$$
$$x = £6.75$$

Q How many parts can a ratio have?

B Proportion

1 If measurements are in direct proportion, this means that as one increases, the other increases by the same percentage.

2 Money is changed from one currency to another using the method of proportion.

3 In January 2002, the euro became legal tender in many European countries.
- On the day we checked, a euro (€) was worth about 62p. How many euros is £30 worth?
  Divide 30 by 0.62 this gives €48.39 (€48 and 39 cents).
- Change €25 to pounds.
  Multiply 25 by 0.62 = £15.50.

Q Do an Internet search to find out what £50 is worth today in euros.

c   Percentages

> All percentages are fractions over 100.
>
> So $10\% = \dfrac{10}{100} = \dfrac{1}{10}$ of a quantity.

1 Finding a percentage of a quantity

Divide the percentage by 100 and then multiply by the quantity.

Find 12% of £46.

$\frac{12}{100} \times 46 = 5.52 = £5.52$

2 Expressing one quantity as a percentage of another quantity

Calculate 17 000 out of 20 000 as a percentage.

$\frac{17\,000}{20\,000} \times 100\% = 85\%$

3 Increasing a quantity by a percentage

Increase £10 by 30%.

Here £10 is 100%, so we need 130%

$\frac{130}{100} \times 10 = £13$

4 Reducing a quantity by a percentage

Reduce £10 by 40%

Now we need 60% of the original amount.

We have already seen this in type 1:

$\frac{60}{100} \times 10 = £6$

Q Any percentage can be written as a decimal, e.g. 12% = 0.12. How would you write the other percentages in this section on decimals?

These are the four types of percentage question you might be asked in an exam.

PRACTICE

1 Write these ratios as simply as possible:

(a) 8g : 1kg   (b) 125p : £10

2 Convert the following sterling amounts to euros (take €1 as 62p):

(a) £35   (b) £142   (c) £1500

3 Over a period of 8 months a hive of bees increased in number by 25% and then by another 44%. Originally there were 2500 bees; how many are there now?

4 When an iron bar is heated, it increases in length by 0.3%. If the increase in length is 2 cm, what was the original length of the bar?

5 In the last three weeks of a sale, prices were reduced by 25% and then another 30%. What was the final sale price of a coat that originally cost £120?

THE BARE BONES

➤ Certain numbers, such as $\sqrt{2}$, cannot be written down exactly as fractions or decimals. However, you can write down an approximate value. For example, $\sqrt{2} = 1.414213562373$ to 12 d.p).

➤ The only way to write $\sqrt{2}$ exactly is to leave it as a square root. In this form, it is known as a surd.

A Manipulating surds

1 Look at $\sqrt{12}$. How else could you write $\sqrt{12}$?

You could say $\sqrt{12} = \sqrt{4 \times 3}$.

$$= \sqrt{4} \times \sqrt{3}$$

You know that $\sqrt{4} = 2$, so $\sqrt{12} = 2 \times \sqrt{3}$.

You write $2 \times \sqrt{3}$ as $2\sqrt{3}$.

So, $\sqrt{12} = 2\sqrt{3}$. This way of writing $\sqrt{12}$ contains the smallest possible number inside the square root sign.

2 Look at $\sqrt{18}$.

$$\sqrt{18} = \sqrt{9 \times 2}$$
$$\sqrt{9} = 3$$
So $\sqrt{9 \times 2} = 3\sqrt{2}$

Q Can you explain how to manipulate a surd to another person?

B More on surds

1 Simplify $\dfrac{\sqrt{20}}{4}$.

$$\frac{\sqrt{20}}{4} = \frac{\sqrt{4} \times \sqrt{5}}{4}$$
$$= \frac{2 \times \sqrt{5}}{4}$$
$$= \frac{\sqrt{5}}{2}$$

2 Simplify $2\sqrt{3} - \sqrt{12}$.

$$= 2\sqrt{3} - \sqrt{4} \times \sqrt{3}$$
$$= 2\sqrt{3} - 2\sqrt{3}$$
$$= 0$$

Q Can you see where you generated the zero from in the second example?

B

3 Simplify $\sqrt{8} \times \sqrt{18}$.

$$\sqrt{8} \times \sqrt{18} = \sqrt{8 \times 18}$$

$$= \sqrt{144}$$

$$= 12$$

C **Rules for surds**

1 There are certain rules that you must learn and understand:

$\sqrt{xy} = \sqrt{x} \times \sqrt{y}$ For example, $\sqrt{12} = \sqrt{6} \times \sqrt{2}$

$\sqrt{\frac{x}{y}} = \sqrt{x} \div \sqrt{y}$ For example, $\sqrt{\frac{7}{3}} = \sqrt{7} \div \sqrt{3}$

$x\sqrt{y} \pm z\sqrt{y} = (x \pm z)\sqrt{y}$ For example, $3\sqrt{2} + 4\sqrt{2} = 7\sqrt{2}$

$$8\sqrt{5} - 3\sqrt{5} = 5\sqrt{5}$$

Q What happens to this rule if *x* or *y* is zero?

2 Remember that for non-zero values of x and y:

$$\sqrt{x} \pm \sqrt{y} \neq \sqrt{x \pm y}$$

PRACTICE

1 Simplify:

(a) $\sqrt{24}$ (b) $\sqrt{28}$ (c) $\sqrt{18} - 3\sqrt{2}$ (d) $\dfrac{\sqrt{8}}{\sqrt{2}}$

2 Simplify:

(a) $7\sqrt{3} - 2\sqrt{3}$

(b) $\sqrt{12} - 5\sqrt{3}$

(c) $\sqrt{48} + 2\sqrt{3}$

(d) $\sqrt{12} + \sqrt{32}$

(e) $7\sqrt{2} - 5\sqrt{2}$

THE BARE BONES

➤ Measuring to the nearest whole unit can be inaccurate by up to one half in either direction.

➤ The rule for rounding or approximating is: 'If the digit you are rounding is five or more than five, round up. If the digit is less than five, round down.'

A   Measuring in everyday life

Remember
Rounded numbers are often enough to make rough calculations or estimates.

1 You can use round or **approximate** numbers when you don't need an exact answer. You can round to the nearest whole number, ten, hundred, thousand, etc. (You can also round to a number of decimal places.)

2 This diagram shows the length of a nail.

- Look at the diagram. How long is the nail, to the nearest centimetre?
- In other words, which whole number of centimetres is the nail closest to? You can see that it is closer to 2 cm than to 1 cm.
- So the length of the nail, to the nearest whole centimetre, is 2 cm.
- How does the rounding rule work in this example? The nail is just over 1.7 cm long. The last figure (7) is more than 5, so you round up.

Q Can you estimate and then measure the dimensions of your bedroom?

3 To the nearest 10 feet, how long is the van?

The last figure (the '3' in 23 feet) is less than 5, so we round down. To the nearest 10 feet, the van is 20 feet long.

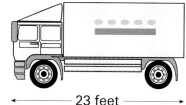

← 23 feet →

B   Using compound measures

KEY FACT

When an object is moving at a **constant speed**:

$$\text{speed} = \frac{\text{distance}}{\text{time}}.$$

Usually the speed of an object is not constant. During a journey the speed varies, so it is only possible to work out the **average speed**:

$$\text{average speed} = \frac{\text{total distance travelled}}{\text{total time taken}}.$$

1 Sometimes you might need to work in two units at the same time. For instance, the speed of a cricket ball can be measured in metres per second.

2 Speed is a measurement that involves a **unit of length** as well as a **unit of time**.

3 Say the cricket ball travels 92 metres in 4 seconds at a constant speed.

4 The cricket ball travels $92 \div 4$ metres every second. This means that the ball travels at 23 metres per second.

Q Can you rearrange the formula for speed to create a formula for time?

C Density

1 Density is another **compound measure** (it has more than one component).

> **Density is defined as the mass of a substance per unit volume.**
> **The formula is density = $\frac{mass}{volume}$.**

2 Find the density of a sheet of corrugated metal that has a mass of 5000 kilogrammes and a volume of 0.75m³.

Following the formula $= \frac{5000}{0.75}$

$\qquad\qquad\quad = 6666.66 \text{ kg/m}^3.$

3 Kg/m³ can also be written as kg m⁻³.

Q Can you estimate the density of your own body?

PRACTICE

1 Look at these objects. Round the lengths of the objects shown to an appropriate unit.

(a)

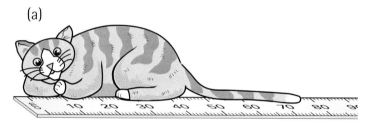

(c)

11.7 cm

(b)

34 feet

(d)

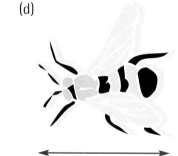

0.236 cm

2 Martin measures the length of a garden fork. The garden fork is 98 cm long.

(a) Estimate the length of the garden fork to the nearest metre.

(b) Estimate the length, in cm, of 3 forks laid end to end.

3 Estimate what 12 kilos of sugar is in pounds, to the nearest pound in weight.

4 Find the average speed of a journey of 250 miles taking five and a half hours to complete.

5 Find the density of a mass of polycarbonate. The mass of the material is 250 kilograms and the volume is 0.75 m³.

THE BARE BONES
- ➤ All formulae for length or distance have one dimension only.
- ➤ All formulae for area have 2 dimensions of length.
- ➤ All formulae for volume have 3 dimensions of length.

A Length

KEY FACT

You can check if a formula is describing length by looking at its <u>components</u>.

1 Consider a square of side length p. The formula for the perimeter is $4p$.

This formula obviously represents a length, because p is a length and 4 is just a number.

2 A rectangle's perimeter will also have a formula for the sum of the lengths of its sides.

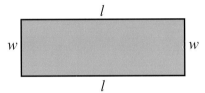

The formula here becomes $2l + 2w$ or $2(l+w)$.

Again, this is a number multiplied by a length.

3 A circle of diameter d units has a perimeter of πd or $2\pi r$.

4 Rob says that the formula $3\pi r$ represents a length, but John argues that it cannot be so. Who is correct?

3 and π are numbers, they do not have a dimension, therefore r is the only element of the formula that does have a dimension. That means this formula is of dimension one, so it **may** be a length.

It is almost certain that there will be a dimension question in the exam. You are usually given a group of formulae, and have to choose the one representing length, area or volume.

Q Can you describe the dimensions of πd?

B Area

Whenever you have a formula for area, you will always have: <u>length × length</u>.

1 The formula for the area of a circle is πr^2.

In the analysis you can ignore π because it is a number and therefore has no dimension, but you do have $r \times r$ in this formula.

2 In other words, you have an area. So the formula is of **dimension two**.

C Volume

All formulae for volume have the dimensions: <u>length × length × length</u>.

1 The formula for the volume of a cylinder is $\pi r^2 h$.

Again we can simply ignore the numbers, in this case π, so the dimensions to consider are r^2 and h.

So this is written as $r \times r \times h$, so it must be a volume.

2 Nisha has these formulae: $5\pi r^2$ $\frac{4}{3}\pi r^3$ $\frac{3}{5}\pi r^2$.

How can she work out which one is a volume?

First of all, ignore the numbers because they do not have dimensions.

So in $5\pi r^2$ we need to consider $r \times r$. This is **dimension two**, so it must be an area.

In $\frac{4}{3}\pi r^3$, we need to consider $r \times r \times r$. This is **dimension three**, so this must be a volume.

1 The letters h and r represent lengths. For each of the following formulae, write down if it represents a length, an area or a volume.

(a) $2\pi r$ (b) πr^2

(c) $\pi r^2 h$ (d) $2\pi r h$

2 The letters l and w represent lengths. Explain why $l^2 l w$ cannot represent an area.

3 Explain what the formula $\frac{4}{3}\pi r^3$ represents.

THE BARE BONES

➤ Area is the amount of surface area covered by a 2-dimensional shape.
➤ Most simple shapes have formulae that can be used to calculate their areas.
➤ More complicated (compound) shapes can be built from simple ones.

A **Rectangles, squares and triangles**

KEY FACT

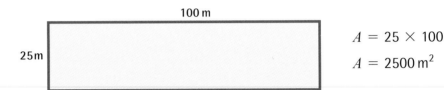

The area of a rectangle = length × width (lw).
The area of a square = length × length (l^2).

1 To find the **area of a rectangle**, use the formula: $A = lw$.

100 m

25 m

$A = 25 \times 100$
$A = 2500 \, \text{m}^2$

Remember
The area of a square is found in a similar way, but you need to use:
$A = l \times l$ (or l^2).

2 Compound shapes can be made by **putting rectangles together**, or removing one rectangle from another.

3 The **area of a triangle** is found by using the **formula**: $A = \frac{1}{2} bh$.

Where b is the base length and h is the height.

l

h

b

Remember
Make sure that you use h and not the slant height l.

KEY FACT

Perpendicular height means the length of the line that forms a **right angle** with the base and passes through a **third vertex** of the triangle.

4 Find the area of a triangle of base length 5 cm and height 12 cm.

$A = \frac{1}{2} \times 5 \times 12$
$= 30 \, \text{cm}^2$

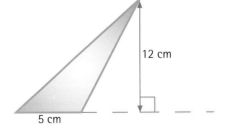

12 cm

5 cm

Q Use this formula to find the area of a triangle that is 11 cm in width and 21 cm in height.

B Parallelograms and trapezia

1 Parallelograms and trapezia both use the perpendicular height in their area formulae:

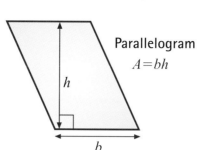

Parallelogram
$A = bh$

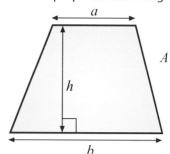

Trapezium
$A = \frac{1}{2}(a+b)h = \frac{(a+b)h}{2}$

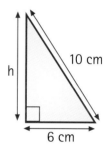

Q Can you explain the connection between the parallelogram formula and the triangle formula?

2 Calculate the area of this trapezium:

The perpendicular height isn't given, so you will have to calculate it using Pythagoras' rule and the triangle on the right.

$h^2 = 10^2 - 6^2$
$= 100 - 36 = 64$

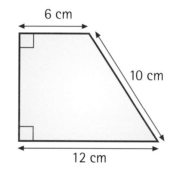

The trapezium formula is usually written out for you at the front of the exam paper.

Using the trapezium formula with $a = 6$ cm, $b = 12$ cm, and $h = 8$ cm gives:

$A = \frac{1}{2}(a+b)h = 72 \text{ cm}^2$

PRACTICE

1 Find the area of this rectangle.

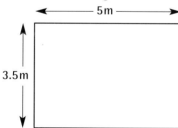

2 Find the area of a carpet needed for this office layout.

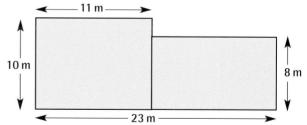

3 Catherine has to paper a bedroom wall that is 3 m high and 10 m long. The wallpaper she wants comes in rolls 2 m wide and 5 m long. How many rolls of paper will she need?

4 Martin wants to paint a fence. The fence is 14 m long and 3 m high. He has to paint both sides of the fence. One tin of paint covers 12 m² of fence. How many tins will he need?

5 Find the area of a triangle that is 6.5 cm in width and 7 cm in height.

6 A trapezium has parallel sides of length 5 cm and 11 cm. Its area is 80 cm². What is its perpendicular height?

THE BARE BONES

➤ Volume is the measure of the amount of space inside a 3-D object, such as a box or a can.

➤ A prism is any solid of uniform cross-section. This means that wherever you cut the solid along its length, it will look the same.

A   Cylinders

Remember
For pi use your calculator π button or 3.142

1 This tin of beans is a good example of a cylinder. If you could cut a tin along its length parallel to its end, the cross section would always look the same, no matter where you cut it.

If you see the word 'uniform' in an exam question, it means 'the same'.

Note that the end of the cylinder (base) is a circle.

KEY FACT

To work out the volume of a cylinder, you use this formula:
volume = area of base $\times$ height
         = $\pi r^2 \times$ height

Remember
Volume is measured in cubic units, that is, cubic metres (m^3) and cubic centimetres (cm^3).

2 Find the volume of a cylinder with a base radius of 4 cm and a height of 10 cm.

Volume = area of base $\times$ height

        = $\pi r^2 \times$ height

        = $\pi \times 4 \times 4 \times 10$

        = 502.7 cm^3 (to 1 decimal place)

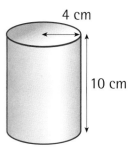

4 cm

10 cm

3 A cylindrical can has a base diameter of 15 cm. The can contains 1 litre of soup. Find the height of the can.

The volume of the cylinder is 1 litre (1000 cm^3).

The radius = 15 cm $\div$ 2 = 7.5 cm

The base area = $\pi r^2 = \pi \times 7.5 \times 7.5 = 176.71\ cm^2$

Volume = area of cross-section $\times$ height

    1000 = 176.71 $\times h$

    $h = \frac{1000}{176.71}$

      = 5.66 cm

Q Can you explain how we arranged the equation to get h on its own?

KEY FACT

<u>Capacity is a measure of the volume of an object</u>. A tank may have a total capacity of 40 litres, but only have 15 litres of fuel actually in it.

B Triangular prisms

Remember
Make sure the units for the height and length are the same – all in centimetres or all in metres.

Q What is the formula for a triangular prism?

The end of this prism is a triangle, so you can use this formula to work out the volume:
volume = area of triangle end × length

1 This triangular prism has:

triangle base = 12 cm,
the triangle height = 10 cm,
and the length of the prism = 21 cm.

2 We can work out the volume using the formula:

3 volume = area cross-section × length

= area of triangle × length

= $\frac{1}{2}$ × 12 × 10 × 21

= 1260 cm^3

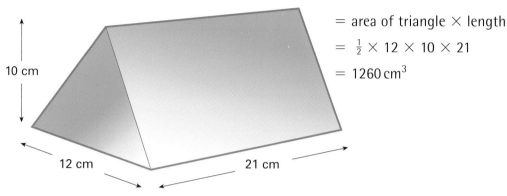

10 cm

12 cm   21 cm

C Cuboids

Q What is the volume of a 6 cm cube?

The volume of a cuboid = length × width × height.

What is the volume of a 20 cm cube?

Volume = width = height = 20 cm

Volume = 20 × 20 × 20 = 8000 cm²

PRACTICE

1 Find the volume of a cuboid of dimensions 2.5 m, 4 m and 6 m.

2 A swimming pool is half full of water. If the dimensions of the pool are 9 m by 12 m by 2 m, how many cubic metres of water are in the pool?

3 Find the volume of a cylinder with a base radius of 10 cm and a height of 12 cm.

4 Julie has a waste bin that is cylindrical in shape. The base has a radius of 0.49 m and the height is 0.82 m. Find the volume of the bin.

5 A kart-racing track has a tunnel shaped like a triangular prism. The dimensions of the tunnel are: 13 m long, 3 m wide and 4 m from its highest point to the ground. Find the volume of the tunnel.

6 A cylindrical time capsule is being placed in a wall for 25 years. The dimensions of the cylinder are: base radius 12 cm, length 100 cm. The hole in the wall has to have 10% more volume than the cylinder. What will the volume of the hole be?

 **Circles 1**

➤ We can use the formulae C = πd and C = 2πr to find the circumference of a circle.

➤ When given the length of the diameter, use C = πd.

➤ When given the length of the radius use C = 2πr.

➤ π is roughly 3.14159265, but it can't be written down exactly.

A Finding the circumference using the diameter

Remember
For diameter, use $C = \pi d$, for radius, use $C = 2\pi r$.

The **circumference** is the distance around the outside of the circle.

A **chord** is the distance across a circle, drawn as a straight line but NOT passing through the centre point.

A chord splits the circle into two **segments**, a minor segment and a major segment.

The **radius** is half of the diameter.

The **diameter** is the distance across a circle, drawn as a straight line from one part of the circumference to another part of the circumference, through the centre point.

A **sector** is a region of the circle bounded by 2 radii and an arc.

1 If you are given the diameter, d, use the formula: $C = \pi d$ (π × diameter).

2 Find the circumference of a circle of diameter 10 cm.

Use the formula: $C = \pi d$
$C = 3.14 \times 10$
$C = 31.4\,cm$

Q Would a circle of twice the diameter have twice the circumference?

B Finding the circumference using the radius

1 If you are given the radius, r, use the formula:

$C = 2\pi r$ (2 × π × the radius)

2 Find the circumference of a circle of radius 12 cm.

Use the formula.

$C = 2\pi r$
$C = 2 \times 3.14 \times 12$
$C = 75.4\,cm$ (to 1 decimal place)

Q Can you use this method to find the circumference of a circle with a radius of 9 cm?

Practice using the value π on your calculator. Don't forget to round to the degree of accuracy the question asks for.

C Finding the area

1 Area is a measure of surface and is always given using square units.

> **To find the area of a circle, use the formula:**
> $A = \pi r^2$ ($\pi \times$ **the radius** $\times$ **the radius**)

2 A stands for area and r stands for radius.

3 Find the area of a circle of radius 15 cm.

Use the formula: $A = \pi r^2$
$$A = \pi \times 15 \times 15$$
$$A = 706.86 \, \text{cm}^2$$

Q How would you find the area of a circle, if you only knew its diameter?

PRACTICE

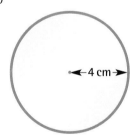

1 Find the circumference of each of the following circles, using the value for π on your calculator or 3.14:

(a) radius 7 cm   (b) diameter 4 cm

(c) diameter 25 cm   (d) radius 10.9 cm

2 Find the areas of the following circles:

(a)   (b)

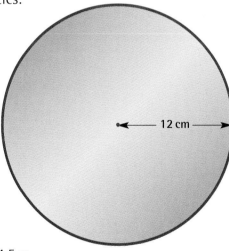

3 A circular pond has a diameter of 4.5 m.

It is surrounded by a path that is 1.2 m wide.

Find:

(a) the area of the pond

(b) the area of the path.

4 A circle has an area of 100 cm², find the radius.

Remember
For question 4, use the formula backwards. Divide by π to find the square of the radius first, then square root it, to find the radius.

THE BARE BONES

➤ You need to know certain facts in order to be able to calculate angles and use angle properties connected with circles.

➤ The lengths of 2 tangents from a point are equal.

➤ The angle between a tangent and a chord is equal to the angle in the alternate segment.

A | **Tangents and chords**

KEY FACT

> When any <u>chord</u> is bisected by its <u>perpendicular bisector</u>, the perpendicular bisector must pass through the centre of the circle.

Remember
The angle between a tangent and a radius is 90°.

1 OX and OY are radii of the circle. This must mean that triangle OXY is an isosceles triangle. So OZ must be a mirror line. In order that XOZ and OZY are mirror images of each other, the angles at Z, which are on a straight line XY, must each be $\frac{1}{2}$ of 180°. Therefore, each angle must be 90°.

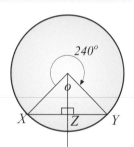

2 Using the knowledge established above, we can find missing angles in circles.

3 We need to find the angles at a and b.
To find b, the angle at O must be 360° − 240° = 120°.
So b must be $\frac{1}{2}$ of 120° = 60°.

Therefore $a = 180° − 60° − 90° = 30°$

4 Find the length of AO.

O is the centre of the circle, so OB is part of the radius. So B is at the half-way point between AC, which means AB must be 8 cm. We use Pythagoras:

$$AO^2 = 8^2 + 6^2$$
$$AO^2 = 64 + 36$$
$$AO = 10 \text{ cm}$$

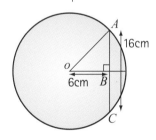

5 The tangents drawn from a point to a circle must be equal.

The centre of the circle is O. This must act as a mirror line. Since OA and OB are radii they must be equal. Therefore, OAC and OBC must be equal. So AC = BC.

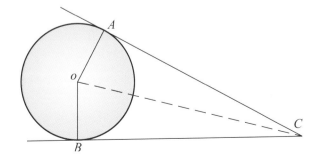

Q Can you explain how to find the perpendicular bisector of a line?

B Angles in semi-circles

1 The triangle in a semi-circle is a right-angled triangle.

We use this fact in more complex questions to find missing angles.

Find the size of the angles at *m* and *n*.

In the triangle, WXZ must be 90° because it is a triangle in a semi-circle. So *m* = 60° (3rd angle in a triangle).

The lines are parallel, so *n* must be equal to *m* = 60°

2 The angle subtended at the centre of a circle is twice the angle subtended by the same arc at any point on the remaining part of the circumference.

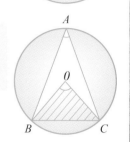

Both of these angles come off the same arc AC. This means that ABC is half the size of AOC, or alternatively AOC is twice the size of ABC.

3 Angles in the same segment are equal.

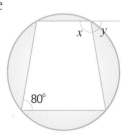

AB is a chord of the circle, this means that C and D lie on the major arc of the chord. From this, we can see that they are in the same segment and are therefore equal.

C Cyclic quadrilaterals

1 Concyclic points are points that lie on the circumference of the same circle. If a **circle can be drawn through all four points of a quadrilateral**, then the quadrilateral is called a cyclic quadrilateral.

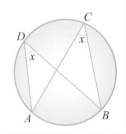

2 Find angles *x* and *y*.

x is opposite 80° in a cyclic quadrilateral and therefore is 100° and *y* is adjacent to *x* on a straight line, and so must be 80°.

1 Find angle *a*.

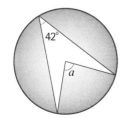

2 Find angles *x*, *y* and *z*.

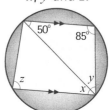

3 Find the missing angles.

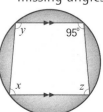

THE BARE BONES

➤ You can use angle facts to find the unknown angles in triangles and to solve other mathematical problems.

➤ Angles that occur when parallel lines are crossed by another line are called alternate angles, corresponding angles or allied angles.

A Angle facts

KEY FACT

1 **Angles on a straight line** add up to **180°**.

$x + y = 180°$

You can use this fact to work out an unknown angle, by subtracting the angle you know from 180°

KEY FACT

2 **Angles around a point** add up to **360°**.

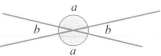

Add the angles that you have and subtract them from 360°. This will give you the size of the unknown angle.

KEY FACT

3 **Angles opposite each other at a vertex are equal.**

In the diagram, the angles marked 'a' are equal and the angles marked 'b' are equal.

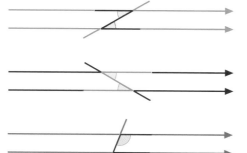

4 **Alternate** angles are known as **Z angles**.

The angles in the crooks of the Z are equal.

The Z may be backwards, as in the second diagram, but the angles in the crooks of the Z are still equal.

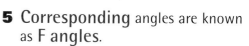

5 **Corresponding** angles are known as **F angles**.

6 **Allied angles** are opposite each other between parallel lines and add up to 180°.

Remember
A scalene triangle has all sides different and all angles different. An equilateral triangle has all sides equal, and all its angles are 60°.

KEY FACT

7 **Angles in a triangle** add up to **180°**.

If angle x is 48°, work out the unknown angles in the triangle shown.

The marks on the lines show that these two sides are equal in length, so it must be an **isosceles triangle**. (An isosceles triangle has two equal sides and two equal angles.)

So the two unknown angles must be equal.

The answer must be: $\frac{180 - 48}{2} = \frac{132}{2} = 66°$.

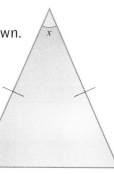

Q Can you explain why you calculated $\frac{180 - 48}{2} = 66°$?

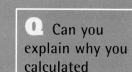

B Finding unknown angles

1 We can find the unknown angles in this triangle using algebra with the angle facts we know.

2 First we set up an equation:

$$x + (x + 3) + (2x + 57) = 180$$
$$4x + 60 = 180$$
$$4x + 60 - 60 = 180 - 60$$
$$4x = 120$$
$$\frac{4x}{4} = \frac{120}{4}$$
$$x = 30$$

So the missing angles are 30°, 33° $(x + 3)$, and 117° $(2x + 57)$.

 What type of triangle is this one?

In an exam question, make sure the angles you calculate in a triangle do add up to 180°.

 **PRACTICE**

1 Find the value of x, in degrees.

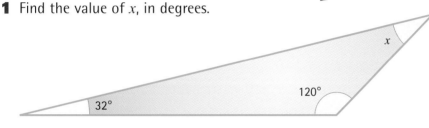

Remember
You will need to set up an equation.

2 The three angles of this triangle are x, $2x$ and $3x$. Find the size of each angle, in degrees.

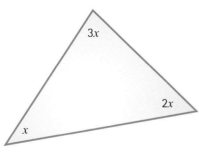

3 Find the unknown angles in this diagram.

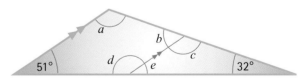

4 ABC is a right-angled isosceles triangle. Find the unknown angles.

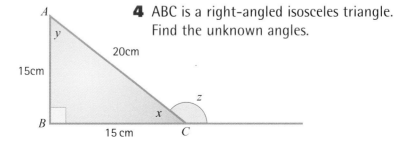

Pythagoras' rule

THE BARE BONES

➤ Pythagoras was a Greek who lived around 500 BC. He discovered a unique fact about right-angled triangles.

➤ Pythagoras' rule: 'The square of the hypotenuse of a right-angled triangle equals the sum of the squares of the other two sides.'

A Which side is the hypotenuse?

1 The hypotenuse is the longest side in a right-angled triangle. It is always **opposite the right angle**.

5 cm 4 cm 3 cm

2 In this triangle, the hypotenuse is 5 cm, as this is the longest side.

3 'The square of the hypotenuse' means the length of the hypotenuse squared. The square of the hypotenuse of this triangle equals $5^2 = 25$.

KEY FACT

> Pythagoras' rule says that this is '<u>equal to the sum of the squares of the other two sides</u>'.

Q How could you check this rule with a drawing?

4 This means that the length of each of the other sides is squared and then they are added together.

Algebraically the rule is written as:

$$h^2 = a^2 + b^2$$
$$= 4^2 + 3^2$$
$$= 9 + 16 = 25 \text{ (the square of the hypotenuse)}$$

h a b

KEY FACT

> Use this rule to find an unknown side in a right-angled triangle.

B Finding the length of the hypotenuse

Remember
Finding unknown sides or angles is called 'solving the triangle'.

1 By using Pythagoras' rule, we can find the length of the unknown side.

x cm 8 cm 6 cm

2 The unknown side of this triangle is x, so we square it, making it x^2. The other two sides squared are 6^2 and 8^2.

3 Using Pythagoras' rule, we can form an equation
$$x^2 = 6^2 + 8^2$$
Work out the right-hand side of the equation
$$x^2 = 36 + 64$$
$$x^2 = 100$$

Q Could a triangle with sides 9 cm and 12 cm have a third side of 16 cm and be a right-angled triangle?

4 Is this the answer to the question? We don't want x^2, we want x. To find this, we need to take the square root of each side of the equation.
$$\sqrt{x^2} = \sqrt{100}$$
$$x = 10 \text{ cm}$$

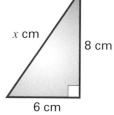

You might see the word 'theorem', e.g. Pythagoras' theorem. It means 'rule'.

C An example using decimals

1 In some triangles, the lengths of the sides are not easy-to-use whole numbers. Sometimes they involve decimals.

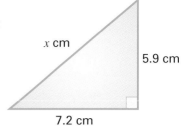

x cm

5.9 cm

7.2 cm

2 Pythagoras' rule still works.

$x^2 = 7.2^2 + 5.9^2$
$x^2 = 51.84 + 34.81$
$x^2 = 86.65$

3 Now take the square root of both sides of the equation.

$x = 9.308598176\ldots$
$x = 9.31$ cm (to 2 decimal places)

Q Find the hypotenuse of a right-angled triangle with base 10 cm and height 5 cm, to 1 d.p.

D Finding other missing sides

1 Here, we have an unknown side that is not the hypotenuse.

5 cm

3 cm

x cm

2 Using Pythagoras' rule: $5^2 = 3^2 + x^2$

3 Try to solve the equation. We need to rearrange the equation to get x on its own, with all the other numbers on the other side of the equation. We do this by taking 3^2 away from both sides:

$5^2 - 3^2 = 3^2 + x^2 - 3^2$.

4 On the right side, 3^2 is subtracted, leaving only the x^2.

5 Now the equation reads as: $5^2 - 3^2 = x^2$ (This is exactly the same as $x^2 = 5^2 - 3^2$)
$25 - 9 = x^2$
$16 = x^2$
$x = 4$ cm

6 Since the triangle is a 3, 4, 5 triangle, this is the result that we would expect.

Remember
You have to find the square root of x to find the answer.

Q What are the base and height of an isosceles right-angled triangle with hypotenuse 10 cm?

PRACTICE

Find x in the following triangles.

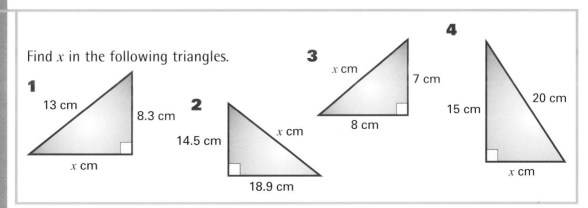

1 13 cm, 8.3 cm, x cm

2 14.5 cm, x cm, 18.9 cm

3 x cm, 7 cm, 8 cm

4 15 cm, 20 cm, x cm

THE BARE ➤ You can solve problems by using Pythagoras' rule.

BONES ➤ When the rule is applied to solving problems, you need to draw the right-angled triangle and put in the measurements. This will give you a diagram from which you can work.

A   Finding the diagonal of a rectangle

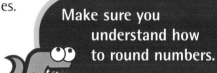

Find the length of the diagonal of a rectangle that is 8 cm long and 5 cm wide.

Remember
Pythagoras is often incorrectly linked with trig. Don't confuse them.

Step 1:   Drawing a diagram of the shape makes the question easier to understand.

Step 2:   You can see from the diagram that this is still a right-angled triangle question, so you simply apply Pythagoras' rule in the same way.

Let the diagonal be x cm

KEY FACT

> When allocating a name to an unknown quantity, you usually use x.

Q Use this method to find the length of the diagonal of a rectangle, with length 10 cm and width 4 cm.

$x^2 = 8^2 + 5^2$

$x^2 = 64 + 25$

$x^2 = 89$ Take the square root of both sides.

$x = 9.433981132$

$x = 9.43$ (to 2 decimal places)

The diagonal is 9.43 cm (to 2 decimal places).

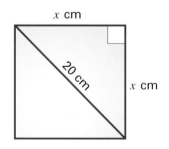

Make sure you understand how to round numbers.

B   Finding the unknown side of a square

A square has diagonals 20 cm in length.

Find the length of one side of the square.

Step 1:   Draw the diagram.

Step 2:   Use Pythagoras' rule.

You know that the sides of a square are the same length. Let the sides be x cm.

$20^2 = x^2 + x^2$

$400 = 2x^2$ Divide both sides of the equation by 2.

$200 = x^2$ Take the square root of both sides of the equation, putting x on the left-hand side for neatness.

$x = 14.14213562$

$x = 14.14$

The diagonal is 14.14 cm (to 2 decimal places)

c   Problems involving decimals

A rectangular field has one side of 8.2 m
and a diagonal of 12.4 m.
Find the length of the missing side.

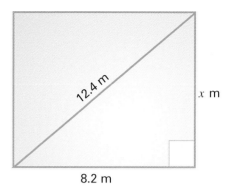

Step 1:   Draw the diagram.

Step 2:   Use Pythagoras' rule.

$$12.4^2 = x^2 + 8.2^2$$
$$153.76 = x^2 + 67.24$$

Subtract 67.24 from both sides. This will leave the x^2 term on its own on the
right-hand side of the equation.

$$153.76 - 67.24 = x^2 + 67.24 - 67.24$$
$$86.52 = x^2$$

Now take the square root of both sides. For neatness, put the x on the left-hand side.

$$x = 9.301612763 \ldots$$
$$x = 9.30 \, \text{m}$$

The result is 9.30 m (to 2 decimal places).

**A square has
diagonals of
length 15 cm.
Can you use the
method to find
the length of
the sides?**

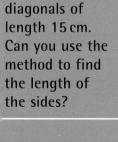
PRACTICE

Remember
Draw diagrams
to help you
answer these
questions.

1 A 5 m ladder rests against a wall with its foot 2 m from the wall. How far up the
wall does the ladder reach?

2 A plane flies 30 km north and then 40 km west. How far away is it from its
starting point?

3 An army platoon travels 42.43 km on a bearing of 045 degrees. Then they travel on
a new bearing of 180 degrees for a distance of 30 km. How far away are they from
their original starting point?

4 Martha and Prakash were arguing about a triangle that had sides of 9 cm, 12 cm
and 15 cm. Prakash said the triangle had a right angle. Martha said it did not.
Who was correct?

5 A piece of curtain material is a rectangle of length 2.5 m and width 1.6 m.
How long is the diagonal?

6 Find the distance between each pair of co-ordinate points, rounding to 1 d.p.
where necessary.

(a) (0,7) and (7,0)   (b) (1,4) and (8,8)   (c) (3,3) and ($-$2,1)

THE BARE BONES

➤ Trigonometry involves understanding ratios between the sides of right-angled triangles.

➤ You need to set up equations and solve them to find unknown sides or angles.

➤ There are three ratios to understand in right-angled triangles: sine, cosine and tangent ratios.

A Trig ratios

1 In trigonometry, the sides of a right-angled triangle are given temporary labels in relation to one of the angles:

2

KEY FACT

The ratios of these sides to each other are the trigonometrical (trig) ratios of the angle x.

The ratios have the following names and abbreviations:

- the sine of x ($\sin x$) = $\dfrac{\text{opposite}}{\text{hypotenuse}}$

- the cosine of x ($\cos x$) = $\dfrac{\text{adjacent}}{\text{hypotenuse}}$

- the tangent of x ($\tan x$) = $\dfrac{\text{opposite}}{\text{adjacent}}$

Q Why does the tangent of 40° always have the same value, whatever the size of the triangle?

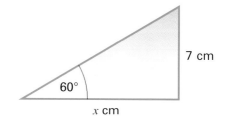

Your calculator may have different angle modes, such as radians or grades, which will make your trig keys give incorrect results. Check the mode is set to degrees, by testing $\sin 30° = 0.5$.

B Finding a missing side

Remember
Ask yourself 'Do I need sin, cos or tan?'

1 Find the length of the side marked x in the triangle.

$\sin 32° = \frac{x}{12}$

12 cm

x cm

32°

2 Multiply both sides by 12

$12 \times \sin 32° = x$

$x = 6.359031171$

$x = 6.36$

Q If the adjacent side is missing, which ratio would you use?

3 $\tan 60° = \frac{7}{x}$

$x \tan 60° = 7$

$x = \dfrac{7}{\tan 60°}$

$= 4.04$ cm to 2 d.p

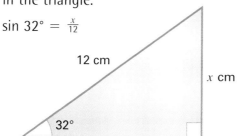

7 cm

60°

x cm

C *Finding an unknown angle*

On your calculator you will find keys marked sin^{-1}, cos^{-1} and tan^{-1}. You might have to press a shift or inverse button first.

1 Find the size of angle θ.

2 Use sin.

$\sin \theta = \frac{15}{30}$

$\sin \theta = 0.5$

$\theta = \sin^{-1} 0.5$

$\theta = 30°$

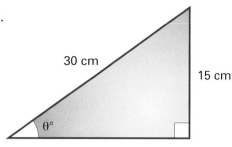

30 cm   15 cm   θ°

Q What happens if you try to calculate sin^{-1} 1.5?

Sin^{-1} means 'the angle whose sine is . . .' You might have used a different notation, such as, arc sin.

1 Use your calculator to find the following values:

(a) sin 15°　　　　(b) cos 48°　　　　(c) tan 56°

2 Work out the value of θ when:

(a) sin θ = 0.515　　(b) cos θ = 0.5746　　(c) tan θ = 0.90

3 Find *x*.

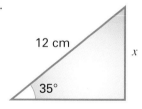

12 cm   *x*   35°

4 Find *y*

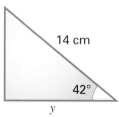

14 cm   42°   *y*

5 The diagram shows a ramp, with an incline of 20°.

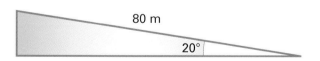

80 m   20°

How high is the ramp?

6 Find the missing angles in these triangles (not to scale):

(a)　　　　　(b)　　　　　(c)　　　　　(d)

14 cm　*z*　30 cm

12.5 cm　25 cm　*y*

18 cm　*m*　19.5 cm

22 cm　*x*　42 cm

Solving simple equations

THE BARE BONES

➤ To rearrange an equation add or subtract, or multiply or divide the same quantity from both sides.

➤ Whatever you do to one side of the equation, you must do exactly the same to the other side.

➤ To 'undo' an operation, perform the opposite or inverse operation.

A **Solving equations with an unknown on one side**

KEY FACT

An equation is like a puzzle. Finding the correct value for the letter in an equation solves the puzzle. This value is the solution to the equation.

Remember
$3x$ means $3 \times x$, so to remove the 3 you need to divide 3.

1 You can solve this equation: $3x + 4 = 19$

$$3x + 4 - 4 = 19 - 4 \quad \text{First take 4 from both sides.}$$
$$3x = 15$$
$$\frac{3x}{3} = \frac{15}{3} \quad \text{Now divide both sides by 3.}$$
$$\text{So } x = 5$$

2 Solve $5x - 1 = 34$

$$5x - 1 + 1 = 34 + 1 \quad \text{Add 1 to both sides.}$$
$$5x = 35$$
$$\frac{5x}{5} = \frac{35}{5} \quad \text{Divide both sides of the equation by 5.}$$
$$\text{So } x = 7$$

Q Can you define the coefficient of x?

Always work through your solution one step at a time. Trying to do too much at once can cause mistakes.

B **Solving equations with unknowns on both sides**

Look at this equation: $4x - 6 = 3x + 3$

Step 1: Remove the x term from the right-hand side.

$$4x - 6 - 3x = 3x + 3 - 3x \quad \text{Subtract } 3x \text{ from both sides.}$$
$$x - 6 = 3$$

Step 2: Remove the number term from the left-hand side.

$$x - 6 + 6 = 3 + 6 \quad \text{Add 6 to both sides.}$$
$$x = 9$$

Q Use this method to solve these equations:

(a) $2y + 5 = y + 9$

(b) $9k + 8 = 45k$

C *Where the x term contains a fraction*

There are two cases:
either the unknown is the denominator of the fraction, or the numerator.

$\frac{x}{5} - 7 = 10$

$\qquad \frac{x}{5} = 10 + 7$ $\quad (+7$ to both sides$)$

$\qquad \frac{x}{5} = 17$

$\qquad x = 85$ $\qquad (\times$ both sides by 5$)$

$\frac{2}{x} + 3 = 7$

$\qquad \frac{2}{x} = 7 - 3$ $\quad (-3$ from both sides$)$

$\qquad \frac{2}{x} = 4$

$\qquad 2 = 4x$ $\qquad (\times$ both sides by $x)$

$\qquad 0.5 = x$ $\qquad (\div$ both sides by 4$)$

Q Can you explain how we got an answer of 85?

D *Equations with a negative x term*

1 This equation has a **negative unknown** on one side: $5 - 6x = 3$

$\qquad 5 - 6x + 6x = 3 + 6x \qquad$ add $6x$ to both sides

$\qquad\qquad 5 = 3 + 6x$

$\qquad 5 - 3 = 3 + 6x - 3 \qquad$ subtract 3 from both sides

$\qquad\qquad 2 = 6x$

$\qquad\qquad \frac{2}{6} = \frac{6x}{6}$

$\qquad$ So $x = \frac{1}{3}$

Remember
Check the answer by substituting into the original equation.

2 Solve $5x + 2 = 1 - x$

$\qquad 5x + 2 + x = 1 - x + x \qquad$ add x to both sides

$\qquad\qquad 6x + 2 = 1$

$\qquad 6x + 2 - 2 = 1 - 2 \qquad$ subtract 2 from both sides

$\qquad\qquad 6x = -1$

$\qquad\qquad \frac{6x}{6} = \frac{-1}{6}$

$\qquad\qquad x = \frac{-1}{6}$

Q Use this method to solve these equations:

(a) $-9n = 12$

(b) $1 - 4r = -2r$

Align the equal signs in your working. It makes your answer look neater and it is easier to read your working.

PRACTICE

Solve these equations and check your answers.

1 $3x + 2 = 23$

2 $5y + 7 = 52$

3 $8d + 3 = 19$

4 $10f + 7 = 127$

5 $6c - 1 = 5c + 4$

6 $7h - 3 = 11h - 5$

7 $4x + 5 = 10x - 13$

8 $3x + 7 = 3 - x$

9 $9 - \frac{1}{3}k = 2k - 5$

10 $4 - 8p = 2 - 5p$

Rearranging formulae

➤ Rearranging formulae means getting the subject on one side of the equals sign and everything else on the other side of the equals sign.

➤ It is also known as changing the subject, or transformation of formulae.

A Changing the subject – types 1 and 2

KEY FACT

Changing the subject of a formula means rearranging a formula to get one letter on its own and all of the other letters on to the other side of the equals sign.

Remember
The plural of formula is 'formulae', but you might see it written as 'formulas' in the exam.

1 It is also known as **transformation** of formulae.

Type 1: When x is not 'bound' up with anything else:

$$x + a = b$$
$$x + a - a = b - a \quad \text{here subtract } a \text{ from both sides}$$
$$x = b - a$$

Type 2: When x is 'bound' in a multiplication:

$$xy = a$$
$$\frac{xy}{y} = \frac{a}{y} \quad \text{divide both sides by } y$$
$$x = \frac{a}{y}$$

2 Look at this formula: $2x^2y = z$

$$\frac{2x^2y}{2y} = \frac{z}{2y} \quad \text{divide both sides by } 2y$$
$$x^2 = \frac{z}{2y} \quad \text{now cancel the } 2y\text{s on the left}$$
$$x = \sqrt{\frac{z}{2y}} \quad \text{remove the square by finding the square root of both sides}$$

Q Make x the subject of this formula:

$$x + y = p$$

B Combinations of types 1 and 2

Remember
The equals signs should be directly under each other.

1 Make x the subject of this formula:

$$q + 6x = p$$
$$q + 6x - q = p - q \quad \text{isolate the } x\text{s first by taking } q \text{ from both sides}$$
$$6x = p - q$$

2 We need only one x on the left-hand side, so we 'undo' $6x$ by dividing each side by 6: $x = \frac{p-q}{6}$

Q How else could $\frac{p-q}{6}$ be written?

C What to do if the subject has a minus sign

1 Sometimes you may arrange a formula only to find that the left-hand side contains the subject with a minus sign in front of it, for example $-A = sx - 2t$.

> **If this happens, multiply both sides of the equation by -1.**

This has the effect of changing the sign of **every term** in the formula, because: $-A \times -1 = A$.

If $-A = sx - 2t$, then $A = -sx + 2t$

2 Make r the subject of $3M - 2r = 4N$.

$-2r = 4N - 3M$	subtract $3M$ from both sides
$-r = 2N - \frac{3M}{2}$	divide both sides by 2
$r = -2N + \frac{3M}{2}$	multiply both sides by -1
$r = \frac{3M}{2} - 2N$	rearrange right-hand side for neatness

Q Make d the subject of:

$u + v - d = 0$

D When factorisation is required

1 If the letter you want to make the subject of a formula occurs in **two terms**, you may need to **collect** these terms and then **factorise** them.

> Make sure you show your working. It is important to let the examiner see how you have worked out the answer.

2 Make x the subject of $2x = px + q$.

$2x - px = q$	subtract px from both sides
$(2 - p)x = q$	factorise the left-hand side
$x = \frac{q}{2-p}$	divide both sides by $2-P$

Q Make n the subject of:

$W + sn = tn$

In these questions, make x the subject of the formula.

1 $x + 9 = r$ **2** $x - z = a$

3 $5x + 4y = 16$ **4** $mx^2 = c$

5 $\frac{1}{4}x = m$ **6** $\frac{x}{p} = p + c$

7 $\frac{mx}{b} = c$ **8** $5 - fx = 3x + p$

In these questions, make y the subject of the formula.

9 $2x + 5y = 9$ **10** $x - 2y = 10$

Remember

In question 5, $\frac{1}{4}x$ is the same as $\frac{x}{4}$

THE BARE BONES

➤ An inequality is a mathematical statement describing a range of values.

➤ Inequalities can be shown on a number line.

➤ To solve inequalities using algebra you apply the same techniques used in equations and rearranging formulae.

A *Showing inequalities on a number line*

There are four inequality symbols:

> greater than	≥ greater than or equal to
< less than	≤ less than or equal to

KEY FACT

You can use a number line to show an inequality.

Remember
We usually assign a letter to indicate the variable, e.g. x.

1 We can show $x > 4$, which means x is greater than 4:

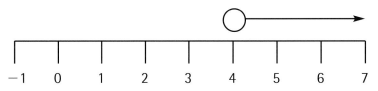

KEY FACT

The empty circle means the value of 4 is not included in the inequality.

2 Here is $x \leqslant 3$:

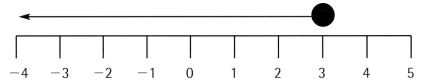

KEY FACT

Here the filled circle means that $x = 3$ is included.

3 Look at this line:

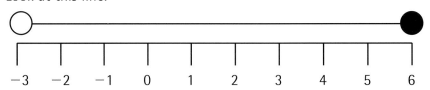

Q Can you think of another way to describe this inequality in words?

This line shows $-3 < x \leqslant 6$, this means -3 is less than x, which is less than or equal to 6.

B Solving inequalities

You can solve equations to find an unknown number.
You can solve inequalities to find a range of numbers.

Remember
Do the same thing to both sides of an inequality. If you multiply or divide by a negative number, the direction of the inequality is reversed.

1 So $4 > -5$ is an inequality and it is a true statement.

But what happens if you:

(a) add 5 to both sides?   (b) subtract 3 from both sides?

(c) multiply both sides by 6?   (d) divide both sides by 2?

(e) multiply both sides by -4 (f) divide both sides by -2?

Investigate each of these statements and convince yourself.

You should find that when you multiply or divide by a negative quality, the sense of the inequality is **reversed**.

2 To work out this inequality:

$$4x + 5 > 29 \qquad \text{Subtract 5 from both sides}$$

$$4x + 5 - 5 > 29 - 5$$

$$4x > 24 \qquad \text{Divide both sides by 4}$$

$$\frac{4x}{4} > \frac{24}{4}$$

$$x > 6$$

3 This is a bit more complex.

$$-3 \leqslant 4x + 5 < 12$$

Treat this as two inequalities.

Step 1	Work out $-3 \leqslant 4x + 5$	the answer is $-2 \leqslant x$.
Step 2	Work out $4x + 5 < 12$	the answer is $x < \frac{7}{4}$.
Step 3	Put them together	the final answer is $-2 \leqslant x < \frac{7}{4}$.

Q Can you explain why we divided both sides by 4 in the second step?

PRACTICE

Solve these inequalities.

1 $2x + 7 \geqslant 3x + 2$

2 $7x + 3 > 5x - 4$

3 $8 - 6a \leqslant 7$

4 $1 - 6t \leqslant 9$

5 $-6d < 30$

6 $-2w \geqslant 5$

7 $\frac{1}{4}f + 3 \geqslant 1$

8 $6 > 2p + 3 > 4$

9 $1 \leqslant 5r + 2 \leqslant 12$

10 $-3 < \frac{1}{3}t + 2 < 5$

THE BARE BONES

➤ Straight lines and their equations have common characteristics.

➤ They are all of the form **y = mx + c**, where **m** is the gradient of the line and **c** is the **y-intercept**.

➤ Gradients and **y**-intercepts of lines tell you what type of lines they are.

A Gradients and y-intercepts

Remember
The y-axis on a graph is where $x = 0$.

1 Look at this graph.
It shows the equations:

$y = 2x + 4$ $y = 2x + 2$

$y = 2x + 3$ $y = 2x + 1$

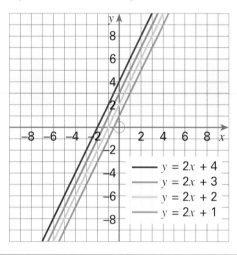

KEY FACT

Q If lines are parallel, what does that tell you about their equations?

All four lines are parallel. Notice that the number in front of the x is 2 in each case (this is the **coefficient** of x). This is the **gradient** of the line. The second number in the equation gives the y-coordinate of the point where the line cuts the y-axis. This point is called the **y-intercept**.

> Given the equation, we can find the y-intercept by substituting $x = 0$ into the equation.

2 Example: In the equation, $y = 3x + 2$, the y-axis is where $x = 0$. So the y-intercept is at:
$y = (3 \times 0) + 2$ or more simply (0, 2).

B Some examples

Make sure you are clear on how to substitute into the equation to find the y-intercept.

1 $y = 9x - 5$

Remember
A graph with a negative gradient slopes from top left to bottom right.

Write down:

(a) the gradient – this is the coefficient of x (the number in front of the x and consequently this must be 9).

(b) the y-intercept of the line – this is where the line cuts the y-axis. The y-axis is the line where $x = 0$. By substituting $x = 0$ into the equation, we can calculate the value of y. This means that y is −5.

So the y-intercept is at (0, −5)

2 $y = -5x + 7$

Write down:

Q What is the gradient of the line $x = 7$?

(a) the gradient – again the gradient is the coefficient of x, so it is −5

(b) the y-intercept of the line – put zero into the equation, for x and the y-intercept is (0, 7).

B

3 A is the point (2, 3), B is the point (4, 4). Find the equation of the line that passes through these points.

The gradient, m, is the measure of the slope. To work this out use the equation:

$$m = \frac{\text{increase in } y \text{ values}}{\text{increase in } x \text{ values}}$$

$$m = \frac{4 - 3}{4 - 2}$$

$$m = \frac{1}{2}$$

To find c you substitute what you know into $y = mx + c$

$$y = \tfrac{1}{2}x + c$$

You have the values of x and y from the points the line passes through.
Using (2, 3) we can say $3 = \tfrac{1}{2} \times 2 + c$

Solving this equation gives us $c = 2$ So your required equation is $y = \tfrac{1}{2}x + 2$

Q Can you use the point (4, 4) to check the equation?

C *Drawing graphs of equations*

1 Draw the line with the equation $y = 2x + 1$

Remember
Two points are enough to draw a straight line, but a third helps, because it checks the line's accuracy.

2 Work out three points   when $x = 1$, $y = (2 \times 1) + 1$
$$= 2 + 1 = 3$$

when $x = 2$, $y = (2 \times 2) + 1$
$$= 4 + 1 = 5$$

when $x = 3$, $y = 7$

So the 3 points are (1, 3), (2, 5), (3, 7).

3 Write down the equation of the line parallel to $y = 2x + 1$, whose intercept is (0, −3)

Q How do you find the equation of a line parallel to a known line, if you know the y-intercept?

The line parallel to $y = 2x + 1$, with a y-intercept (0, −3) is a line with the same gradient, so it must have a 2 in front of the x and it must cut the y axis at −3.
This means that the equation of the line must be $y = 2x − 3$.

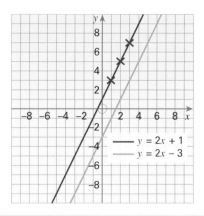

PRACTICE

Write the gradient and the y-intercept of lines with the following equations:

1 $y = 7x + 3$ **2** $y = 3x − 5$ **3** $y = \tfrac{1}{3}x + 12$

4 $y = 3x − 2$ **5** $3x + y = 4$ **6** $2x − y = 7$

7 The gradient of a line is 4 and its y-intercept is (0,5). What is the equation of the line?

8 A line passes through (0,6) and (2,8). Find the equation of the line.

9 Find the equation of the line that passes through the point (0,1) and is parallel to $y = 2x − 1$.

THE BARE BONES

➤ Simultaneous equations are two equations with more than one unknown, usually called x and y, in both equations.

➤ As the equations are simultaneous and linear, you know they form straight lines and the lines cross. The values of x and y are the same in both equations at the point where the lines cross. So the point gives the solution to both equations.

A Graphing simultaneous linear equations

KEY FACT

If a pair of simultaneous linear equations has a solution, their graphs must cross somewhere.

Remember
In algebra, substitution means that a letter is replaced by a number.

1 Write down 3 pairs of integer values which satisfy the equation:

$x + y = 8$

You can have any two values that add to 8.
For instance, you can have:

$x = 1, y = 7$
$x = 2, y = 6$
$x = 3, y = 5$ and so on.

2 Which of the following points lies on the line whose equation is $y = 2x + 1$

(a) (3, 2)   (b) (0, 1)   (c) (3,7)?

Substitute each of these values into the equation in turn:

(a) (3, 2) when $x = 3$, $y = 2(3) + 1$, $y = 7$

This means that (3, 7) is a point on the line, so (3, 2) cannot be a point on the line.

When $x = 0$, $y = 2(0) + 1 = 1$, so (0, 1) is a point that lies on the line.

Q Can you draw graphs of:
$y = 2x + 1$
and:
$y = 21 - 2x$
and show that they are simultaneous equations?

3 Draw the graphs of:
$y = 4 - x$ and $6y = 12 - 2x$
Using your graph, find solutions to the equations.

From the graph, you should be able to see that the lines cross where $x = 3$ and $y = 1$. This means that the coordinates of this point are the solutions to the equations.

In other words, the solutions to the equations are $x = 3$ and $y = 1$

KEY FACT

The point where the two lines cross is the only point that is on both lines. So there is only one point that satisfies both equations. <u>The coordinates of this point provide the solutions to both equations</u>.

B   Using graphs to find solutions – an example

1 *Bitesize Electronics* sells computers.

You can either pay £50 per month or you can pay £600 initially and then £30 per month.

Call the total amount paid p and the time to pay in months t.

2 Form two equations and draw a graph showing payments for up to 3 years.

- $p = 50t$ and $p = 600 + 30t$ are the two equations.
- Now draw the graph.
- Plot the two equations on the graph.

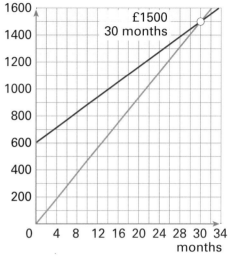

3 Use the graph to work out the cost of a computer and the number of months the customer will need to pay for it.

- You can see from the graph that the lines cross at £1500 after 30 months. This is the total for the computer.
- So the final answer is £1500 and 30 months.

PRACTICE

1 Draw the graphs of $x + y = 10$ and $2x + y = 13$ and solve both equations.

2 Graylaw motors hires cars for a fee of £15 + £5 per day. Judelaw cars hires cars for £7.50 per day. Call the cost of the car hire C. Write two equations to show the cost of hiring from both companies. Draw graphs of each of the equations. Use your graphs to find the number of days for which the cost of hiring is the same for both companies.

3 A business wants to have some leaflets printed. Jayprintwell charges £c cost to print x booklets by using this equation: $c = 75 + 0.1x$. Chargelightly printers say they will charge £15 + 30p per booklet.

(a) Draw a graph to find the number of booklets that both companies would charge the same to produce.

(b) Use the graph to find the cost of working out that number of booklets.

THE BARE BONES

➤ By combining equations, it's possible to make one of the unknown letters disappear, leaving you with a simple equation in x or y to solve. This is called elimination.

A The elimination method

1 Sometimes it's possible just to add two equations together and perform an elimination. It's useful to label equations with letters or numbers as you work. Consider these simultaneous equations:

$x - y = 3$ (i)
$x + y = 11$ (ii)

Adding them together gives
$x - y + x + y = 3 + 11$

Simplifying, $2x = 14$.   (iii)
The y's have been eliminated. Solving this equation, $x = 7$.

Substitute for x into (i), to find the value of y
$7 - y = 3$, so $y = 4$
Check: substitute x and y into equation (ii): $7 + 4 = 11$ ✓

KEY FACT

> **Always use one equation for the calculation and the other equation for the check.**

2 The same result can be obtained by subtracting equation (i) from equation (ii).

$x + y - (x - y) = 11 - 3$
$x + y - x + y = 8$
$2y = 8$ (iv)

The x's have been eliminated.
Solving this gives $y = 4$, as before. $x = 7$ follows by substitution.

Q Solve
$x + 2y = 6$
$x - 2y = 10$
this way.

B Multiplying an equation

1 You can only eliminate one of the letters by adding or subtracting equations if the coefficients match. Sometimes, you need to 'force' a match by multiplying one of the equations first.

2 Solve $2m + 3n = 27$ (i)
                        $m + n = 12$ (ii)

Multiply equation (ii) by 2, to match the coefficients of m:
                $2m + 2n = 24$ (iii)

Now subtract equation (iii) from equation (i):
$2m + 3n - (2m + 2n) = 27 - 24$, so $n = 3$

Q Multiply one of the equations to eliminate n instead of m. Check that you get the same solution.

B

Substitute for n into equation (i):
$$2m + 9 = 27$$
$$2m = 18, \text{ so } m = 9$$
Check: Substitute m and n into equation (ii) $9 + 3 = 12$ ✓

KEY FACT

Never forget to carry out the final check, because it will always show up an error if you have made one.

C | *Equations where both coefficients need to be multiplied*

Remember
If you have a graphical calculator, you can do a quick graph check of your solution.

1 Sometimes just multiplying one of the equations isn't enough to get a match. You need to multiply *both* equations. This can occasionally mean that quite large numbers appear in the new equations.

2 Solve $3x + 2y = 46$ (i)
          $2x - 5y = 18$ (ii)

To eliminate x, multiply equation (i) by 2 and equation (ii) by 3:
    $6x + 4y = 92$ (iii)
    $6x - 15y = 54$ (iv)

Equation (iii) − equation (iv):
$19y = 38$, so $y = 2$
Substitute y into equation (i):
    $3x + 4 = 46$
$3x = 42$, so $x = 14$
Check: substitute for x and y in equation (ii): $28 - 10 = 18$ ✓

Q What would you multiply the equations by to eliminate y?

PRACTICE

1 Solve each pair of simultaneous equations:

(a) $x + y = 7$
    $x - y = 3$

(b) $a + b = 11$
    $a - b = 3$

(c) $2m + n = 19$
    $m - n = 8$

(d) $3t + r = 25$
    $t - r = -1$

(e) $3x + 2y = 23$
    $2x + y = 14$

(f) $4c + 2d = 46$
    $3c + 3d = 48$

(g) $2e + f = 31$
    $3e + 2f = 50$

(h) $2p + 2q = 26$
    $3p + q = 43$

(i) $2a + b = 5$
    $a + 3b = 5$

(j) $p + 2q = 8$
    $2p + 3q = 14$

Remember
Solve the equations by eliminating y.

2 The cost of a car service, c pounds, for n hours of servicing is found by using the formula $c = a + bn$. It costs £100 for a 5-hour service and £76 for a 2-hour service. Find the values of a and b.

3 The points with co-ordinates $(1, 3)$ and $(3, \frac{9}{2})$ lie on the line with the equation $ax - by = 2$.

(a) Find the values of a and b.

(b) Find the gradient of the line.

If a variable has a positive coefficient in one equation and a negative coefficient in the other, choose to eliminate the negative one. You're less likely to make a mistake <u>adding</u> equations.

Using brackets in algebra

THE BARE BONES

➤ Expanding brackets means multiplying terms to remove brackets from equations or expressions.

➤ To expand an expression, you need to multiply each term inside the bracket by the term outside the bracket,
e.g. $3(x + y) = 3 \times x + 3 \times y = 3x + 3y$.

A Expanding brackets

KEY FACT

To expand brackets, multiply everything in the bracket by the term outside the bracket.

1 Expand $3(2a + b) = 6a + 3b$

2 Expand $6(y + 3) = 6y + 18$

It is a common mistake to forget to multiply the **second** term.
If you worked out $6y + 3$ for the answer to the second equation, you'd be wrong!

3 Expand $3(2x + 4) = 6x + 12$

This example uses the fact that $3 \times 2x = 6x$.

4 Expand $x(4x + 9) = 4x^2 + 9x$

Notice here that the x is the term outside the bracket and that $x \times x = x^2$.

5 Expand $5x(3x - 2) = 15x^2 - 10x$

Notice that $5x \times 3x = 5 \times 3 \times x \times x = 15x^2$.

Remember
$4x^1 \times x^1$
$= 4x^1 \times x^1$
$= 4x^{1+1}$
$= 4x^2$

Q What would $5x \times 3x^2$ expand to?

B Factorising expressions

KEY FACT

Factorising is the opposite of expanding brackets.
Find the highest common factor (HCF) of all of the terms in the expression you are trying to factorise.
The HCF must appear outside the brackets.

Factorise $4x^2 + 8x$.

1 Here the HCF is the largest term that is a factor of $4x^2$ and $8x$. The HCF must be $4x$.

2 So we now have $4x^2 + 8x = 4x(? + ?)$.

3 Ask yourself, 'What do I multiply $4x$ by, to make $4x^2$, and what do I multiply $4x$ by to make $8x$?'

4 So the final answer $= 4x(x + 2)$.

Q What is the HCF of $15x^2y$ and $20xy^2$?

C Solving equations with brackets

Method 1

1 Solve $4(x + 3) = 28$

2 Expand the brackets:

$$4x + 12 = 28$$

3 Solve it like any other equation:

$$4x + 12 = 28$$
$$4x = 16$$
$$x = 4$$

Method 2

1 Solve $4(x + 3) = 28$

2 $4(x + 3)$ is a product, it is $4 \times (x + 3)$

3 So divide by 4 to undo the multiplication:

$$\frac{4(x + 3)}{4} = \frac{28}{4}$$
$$x + 3 = 7$$
$$x = 4$$

Q Try both methods to solve this equation:

$4(x + 3) = 36$

D Solving equations with two sets of brackets

Solve $3(x + 4) + 5(x - 6) = 5x - 3$.

Step 1: Expand the brackets and simplify.

$$3x + 12 + 5x - 30 = 5x - 3$$
$$8x - 18 = 5x - 3$$

Step 2: Solve the equation. You should find that:

$$x = 5$$

Q Can you explain where the $- 30$ came from in step 1?

PRACTICE

Solve these equations.

1 $2(x + 5) = 18$

2 $5(x - 2) = 40$

3 $4(3x - 7) - 5(2x - 4) = 3x$

4 $2(7x - 7) - 2(4x + 5) = 21 - 4x$

5 $5 + (7x - 7) - 2(4x + 5) = 2x + 4$

6 $6(4x - 7) + 3(13 - 3x) = 20x - 23$

7 $8(2x - 9) - 2(9 - 2x) = 14x + 3$

8 Factorise:
   (a) $14x^2 + 7x$ (b) $36y^2 - 9y$

9 Factorise:
   (a) $15y^4 + 25y^2$ (b) $100a^2 + 20ab^3$

Multiplying bracketed expressions

THE BARE BONES

➤ You need to know how to expand expressions, such as $(w + x)(y + z)$.

➤ Both terms in the first brackets have to be multiplied by both terms in the second, resulting in four new terms.

A **Bracketed expressions**

1 Look at this rectangle.

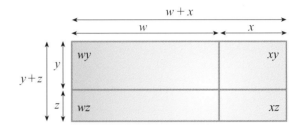

Q Can you use this idea to expand

$(2w + x)(y + z)$?

2 The area of this rectangle is $(w + x)(y + z)$.

3 We can write this as the combined area of the four smaller rectangles:

$wy + wz + xy + xz$

B **More difficult expansions**

1 Expand and simplify:

$(x + 7)(x + 2)$

$= x(x + 2) + 7(x + 2)$

$= x^2 + 2x + 7x + 14$

$= x^2 + 9x + 14$

Remember
Each term in the first bracket is used to multiply everything in the second bracket. So $(x + 7)(x - 2)$ can be written as $x(x - 2) + 7(x - 2)$

2 Expand and simplify:

$(x + 5)(x - 2) = x(x - 2) + 5(x - 2)$

Here we are taking every term in the first bracket and multiplying the second bracket by it, in turn.

$= x^2 - 2x + 5x - 10$

$= x^2 + 3x - 10$

3 Expand and simplify:

$(x + 7)(3 - x) = x(3 - x) + 7(3 - x)$

$= 3x - x^2 + 21 - 7x$

$= 21 - 4x - x^2$

Q Can you explain where the $-x^2$ came from?

C Expanding a squared expression

1 Expand and simplify:

$$(x + 4)^2 = (x + 4)(x + 4)$$
$$= x(x + 4) + 4(x + 4)$$
$$= x^2 + 4x + 4x + 16$$
$$= x^2 + 8x + 16$$

2 Expand and simplify:

$$(x - 9)^2 = x(x - 9) - 9(x - 9)$$
$$= x^2 - 9x - 9x + 81$$
$$= x^2 - 18x + 81$$

Q Could you now expand $(x + 5)^2$?

KEY FACT

In general $(x + a)^2 = x^2 + 2ax + a^2$ and
$(x - a)^2 = x^2 - 2ax + a^2$

D A special expansion

1 Expand and simplify:
$$(x + 9)(x - 9) = x(x - 9) + 9(x - 9)$$
$$= x^2 - 9x + 9x - 81$$
$$= x^2 - 81$$

2 There is a special expansion that you must learn.
It is called the **difference of two squares**.

KEY FACT

In general $(x + a)(x - a) = x^2 - a^2$

You may be given an expression such as $(x^2 - 144)$ and be asked to factorise it, therefore you need to recognise it as a difference of two squares.

In other words, x^2 is a square and 144 is also a square.

The answer here is $(x + 12)(x - 12)$.

Q Use this method to expand and simplify:
$(x + 7)(x - 7)$

PRACTICE

Expand and simplify:

1 $(x + 3)(x + 1)$ **2** $(x + 7)(x + 2)$ **3** $(x + 2)^2$

4 $(x + m)(x + n)$ **5** $(x + 4)(x + 2)$ **6** $(x - a)^2$

7 $(3 - x)^2$ **8** $(a - x)^2$ **9** $(x - y)^2$

10 $(x + 2)(x - 2)$ **11** $(x + 3y)(x - 3y)$ **12** $(6 - x)(x + 6)$

THE BARE BONES

➤ You have seen inequalities on a number line, you can also view them in regions.

➤ A region is an area of 2-D space with *x* and *y* axes, which is used to represent and illustrate the meaning of an inequality.

A   Shaded and unshaded regions

You shade out one region, so that the area you require is the other non-shaded region.

1 The graph shows the region $x > 4$.

2 This is the unshaded part on the right of the line $x = 4$.

3 Every point to the right of the line $x = 4$ satisfies this inequality.

4 The region that is shaded is the unwanted part for $x > 4$.

5 The line is dotted to show that $x = 4$ is not part of the required region.

Q What inequality would describe the shaded region?

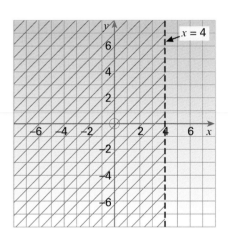

B   Which side of the line satisfies the inequality?

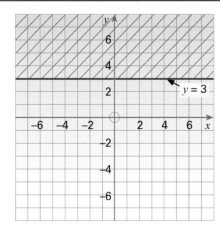

Q Can you use inequalities to describe the rectangle with vertices at (2, −1), (2, 5), (4, 5) and (4, −1)?

1 If it is not obvious which side of the line satisfies the inequality, substitute values of *x* and *y* into the inequality.

2 Use the origin where $x = 0$ and $y = 0$. If the inequality is then satisfied, this is the required region.

3 You need to remember that this area is the one that is **unshaded**.

4 This graph shows $y \leq 3$.

Here the inequality is 'greater than or equal to', so the line is included. This is the reason why the line is solid.

C   Some examples of inequalities and regions

1 The graph shows the region $y < 4x$.

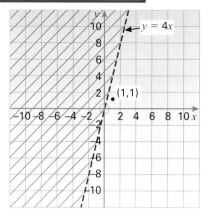

- This line passes through the origin, so you need to test this region by using a different point.

- Substitute the values of x and y, for instance using (1, 1), to see if the equality $y < 4x$ is satisfied.

- Letting $x = 1$ and $y = 1$ does satisfy the inequality $y < 4x$. So the point (1, 1) does lie in the required region.

2

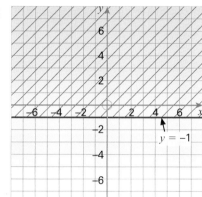

- Here $y \leq -1$ is shown with a solid line.

- So the region we want is below $y = -1$.

Remember
Lines with negative gradients slope from top left to bottom right.

3 Here $y < 5 - x$.

- Look at the line and the region that is shaded. Again this is the region we **do not** want.

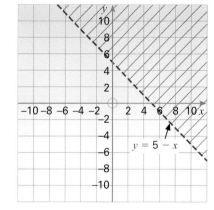

 In the second example why is $y \leq -1$ shown with a solid line?

PRACTICE

Draw diagrams to show the regions that satisfy the inequalities:

1 $x < 3$

2 $y \geq 5$

3 $x \geq 1$

4 $-3 \leq y \leq 3$

5 $y \geq 3 - \frac{x}{2}$

6 $y \geq 3x$

7 $y \leq 3x + 2$

8 $3x - y > 1$

9 $x + 3y > 10$

10 $x + y \geq 1$

THE BARE BONES

➤ You can use a formula to find any term in a sequence.

➤ Given the sequence, you can work backwards and find the formula.

➤ The *n*th term is usually written u_n.

➤ An identity is an algebraic expression where the equality is true for any values of the variable.

A Finding the terms of a sequence

1 The *n*th term of a sequence is given by u_n, e.g. $u_n = 2n + 1$.

• Find the first two terms of this sequence.

Substituting $n = 1$ the first term becomes $u_1 = (2 \times 1) + 1 = 3$

Substituting $n = 2$ $\qquad\qquad\qquad\qquad u_2 = (2 \times 2) + 1 = 5$

• Therefore, the first two terms are 3 and 5.

• Note: $n = 1$ refers to the first term in the sequence and not the value for the first term. Here it shows that term one = 3.

n is called the position of a term in its sequence.

2 For the sequence: $u_n = 12 - 3n$, find u_2:

• Substituting $n = 2$, the second term becomes:
$u_2 = 12 - (3 \times 2) = 6$

• So u_2 is 6.

3 For the sequence: $u_n = 3n^2 + 4$, find the third term in the sequence:

• Substituting $n = 3$, gives:
$3(3^2) + 4 = 31$

• So the third term is 31.

Q What would the third term in the sequence $u_n = 2n + 1$ be?

B Finding which term has a given value

Remember
You will either need to find terms of a sequence or the formula for the sequence.

1 The number 64 is a term in a sequence given by the formula:

$$u_n = 5n + 4$$

2 Which term in the sequence has that value?

3 Substituting $u_n = 64$ into the formula, gives:

$$64 = 5n + 4$$
$$60 = 5n$$
$$n = 12$$

4 So 64 is the 12th term in the sequence.

Q Find the 100th term in the sequence.

C | Finding the formula for a sequence

Q Find the formula for the sequence that begins 4, 9, 14, 19, 24 . . .

1 The first five terms of a sequence are:

7   11   15   19   23

2 Find the nth term.

3 Find the first differences using the table opposite.

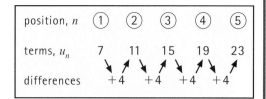

position, n	①	②	③	④	⑤
terms, u_n	7	11	15	19	23
differences		+4	+4	+4	+4

KEY FACT

When the first differences are all equal to a number, a, the formula is $u_n = an + b$, for a suitable value of b.

The terms go up in 4s, so the nth term will be n lots of 4 ($4n$). But the first term is 7, which is 3 more than $4n$.

4 This suggests a formula of $u_n = 4n + 3$, and when tested, you see it works.

D | Identities

Remember
An equation is only true for one value of x.

1 The right-hand side of the equals sign in an identity is just another way of expressing what is written on the left-hand side of the equation.

2 $(x + 3)^2 = x^2 + 6x + 9$

- Substitute 1 into the left-hand side of the equation, you find:

  LHS $= (1 + 3)^2 = 16$

- Now do the same to the right-hand side of the equation $1^2 + 6(1) + 9 = 16$

Q Check to see if the expressions are equivalent: $3x^2 + 4$ and $x^2 + 3x + 2$.

- So both sides are equal. In fact it doesn't matter what value you put in for x, you find that LHS = RHS.

- You should use $\equiv$ for 'equivalent to', so $(x + 3)^2 \equiv x^2 + 6x + 9$

  Often you will see the $=$ sign used instead of the $\equiv$ sign.

PRACTICE

1 Find the first four terms in these sequences:

(a) $u_n = 3n$

(b) $u_n = 2n + 1$

(c) $u_n = 4n - 7$

(d) $u_n = 17 - 2n$

(e) $u_n = 3^n$

(f) $u_n = \frac{2n}{n + 1}$

2 Find the value for n, for which u_n has the given value:

(a) $u_n = 5n + 12$ $u_n = 47$

(b) $u_n = 8(n - 3)$ $u_n = 32$

(c) $u_n = 2n^2 - 4$ $u_n = 158$

3 Find formula for u_n to describe each of these sequences:

(a) 2, 7, 12, 17, . . .

(b) 6, 11, 16, 21, . . .

(c) 9, 17, 25, 33, . . .

(d) 2, 5, 8, 11, . . .

More on formulae

THE BARE BONES

➤ Manipulating formulae is an important skill used in solving equations and solving problems.

➤ Changing the subject means re-arranging a formula to put one unknown on one side and everything else on the other side.

A The difference between a formula and an equation

1 Formulae

$v = \pi r^2 h$ is a formula.

When you substitute in any value of r and h, you can calculate a corresponding value of v. In the same way, if you substitute any value of v, you can find a corresponding value for either r or h.

Look at this formula:

$v = u^2 + 2as$

Find the value of v when $u = 1$, $a = 2$, $s = \frac{1}{2}$

$v = 1^2 + 2(2)(\frac{1}{2})$

So $v = 3$

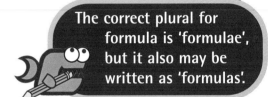

The correct plural for formula is 'formulae', but it also may be written as 'formulas'.

KEY FACTS

A formula applies to an infinite set of data, and can be used to calculate the corresponding value for any given value.

Equations will only hold true for a particular value.

2 Equations

$v = \frac{5}{3}\pi$ is an equation, it is only true for a **particular value** of v ($v = 5.24$ to 2 decimal places).

Q In these last equations example, if $y = +17$, what would the value of x be?

- In the equation, $y = 7x - 3$, find the value of y when $x = -2$

  $y = 7(-2) - 3$

  $y = -17$

- $t = \sqrt{\frac{m}{\pi}}$

  Find t when $m = 10$

  $t = \sqrt{\frac{10}{\pi}}$

  $t = 1.78$ (2 decimal places)

B Manipulating formulae

Sometimes you have to rearrange formulae.

1 Given $v = u + at$, find t when $v = 40$, $u = 5$ and $a = 6$.

Substitute in: $40 = 5 + 6t$

$$6t = 35$$

$$t = 5.83 \text{ (to 2 decimal places)}$$

2 Given $u = 3(x + y)$, find u when $x = 5$ and $y = 7$.

$$u = 3(5 + 7)$$

$$u = 36$$

3 Given $m = \sqrt{\frac{p}{2\pi}}$, find p when $m = 100$

Square both sides to remove the square root sign:

$$m^2 = \frac{p}{2\pi}$$

Now rearrange the formula to make p the subject – multiply both sides by 2π and swap sides:

$$p = 2\pi m^2$$

Now substitute the given value of m:

$$p = 2\pi \times 100^2$$

$$p = 62\,831.85 \text{ (2 decimal places)}$$

Remember
Present answers with reference to their accuracy, i.e. in decimal places or significant figures.

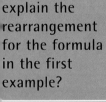 Can you explain the rearrangement for the formula in the first example?

 **PRACTICE**

1 $F = 2(a + b)$ Find F when $a = 4$ and $b = 7$

2 $A = \pi r^2$ Find A when $r = 7.9\,\text{cm}$ (it is area)

3 $c = \pi d$ Find c when $d = 9.3\,\text{cm}$

4 $t = \sqrt{\frac{v}{4\pi}}$ Find v when $t = 12.49$

5 $r = \sqrt{\frac{v}{\pi}}$ Find v when $r = 40$

6 $v = 2\pi\sqrt{\frac{t}{g}}$ Find v when $t = 12$ and $g = 9.8$

7 $s = \frac{1}{2}at^2$ Find t when $s = 100$ and $a = 10$

8 $t = \frac{1}{2}m^2n$ Find m when $t = 144$ and $n = 7$

Quadratic functions

THE BARE BONES

➤ Quadratic functions are functions where the highest power is 2.
➤ The graph of a quadratic function is a parabola.
➤ All parabolas have a line of symmetry.

A Graphing quadratic functions

1 Quadratic expressions are terms that contain a squared term, such as $x^2 - 5$ or $3x^2 + 2x + 5$.

$\frac{1}{2}t(t - 5)$ is also a quadratic because on expansion, you get: $\frac{1}{2}t^2 - 2\frac{1}{2}t$.

2 Draw the graph of $y = x^2$. First make up a table of values.

KEY FACT

> To calculate the values for the table, substitute the values for x into the equation, to find the values of y.

x	−3	−2	−1	0	1	2	3
y	9	4	1	0	1	4	9

Then draw the graph using these points.

Notice that there is a line of symmetry in the graph.

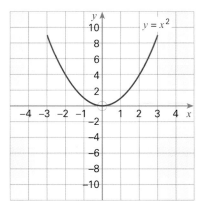

3 Draw the graph of $y = 2x^2$, taking values of x from −3 to +3

Draw up the table:

x	−3	−2	−1	0	1	2	3
x^2	9	4	1	0	1	4	9
y	18	8	2	0	2	8	18

Then draw the graph using these points:

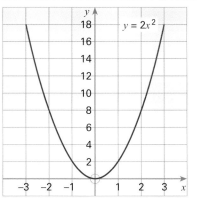

Q Where is the line of symmetry on this graph?

B Some further examples

1 Draw the graph of $y = 2x^2 + 5$ for values of x from -4 to $+4$.

Draw up a table of values:

x	-4	-3	-2	-1	0	1	2	3	4
x^2	16	9	4	1	0	1	4	9	16
$2x^2$	32	18	8	2	0	2	8	18	32
$+5$	$+5$	$+5$	$+5$	$+5$	$+5$	$+5$	$+5$	$+5$	$+5$
y	37	23	13	7	5	7	13	23	37

Draw the graph:

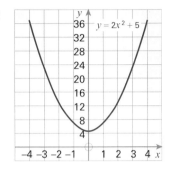

2 Draw the graph of $y = x^2 - 2x - 5$ for values of x from -4 to $+4$.

Draw up a table of values:

x	-4	-3	-2	-1	0	1	2	3	4
x^2	16	9	4	1	0	1	4	9	16
$-2x$	$+8$	$+6$	$+4$	$+2$	0	-2	-4	-6	-8
-5	-5	-5	-5	-5	-5	-5	-5	-5	-5
y	19	10	3	-2	-5	-6	-5	-2	3

To draw a good graph:

Draw the graph:

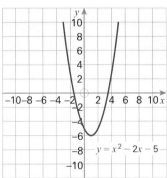

- make sure you have enough points, usually about 8 to 10
- look at the range of values on the x-axis and use this as an indicator on where to site the y-axis, and vice versa
- sketch the curve to get an idea of what it looks like
- draw the curve, put your hand inside the curve to help you get a smooth curve, or draw round a flexi-curve.

PRACTICE

1 Draw the graph of $y = x^2 + 4x + 4$, for suitable values of x.

2 Plot the curve of $y = 3x^2 - 8x + 2$

3 Draw the graph of $y = \dfrac{x(x + 1)}{2}$ Where does the graph meet the y-axis?

THE BARE
BONES
➤ A cubic function is one in which the highest power of x is 3.
➤ Curves of cubic functions usually have a turn in them.
➤ The reciprocal function is $y = \dfrac{1}{x}$

A Drawing up tables and graphs

1 The simplest cubic function is $y = x^3$.

First draw up the table of values:

x	-4	-3	-2	-1	0	1	2	3	4
y	-64	-27	-8	-1	0	1	8	27	64

KEY FACT

The cube of a negative number will itself be negative.

Remember
When you draw
a curve, keep
your hand on
the inside of the
curve to get a
smoother finish,
or use a flexi-
curve.

Now draw the graph:

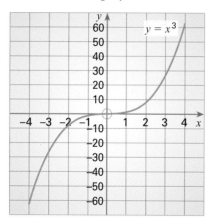

Draw the graph of the curve described
by the equation $y = x^3 + 6x - 4$.
Draw up the table of values:

x	-3	-2	-1	0	1	2	3
y	-49	-24	-11	-4	3	16	41

2 Now draw the graph:

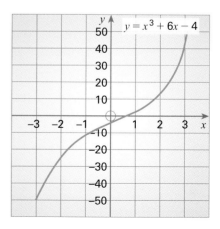

Q What is the
difference
between x^3 and
$3x$?

B The shape of the cubic equation curve

When the coefficient of x^3 is **positive**, the curve can be like the one below. Graphs of the form $y = ax^3$ all have a similar shape to this. When the value of a increases, the shape gets steeper.

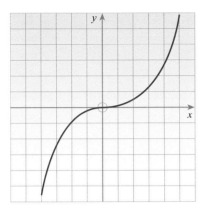

When the coefficient of x^3 is **negative**, the curve can be like the one below. Graphs of the form $y = -ax^3$, where the value of a is negative, have a similar shape as when a is positive but reflected in the y-axis.

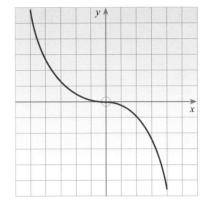

Graphs of the form $y = x^3 + c$ all have a similar shape to the one below. They all cut the y-axis at $(0, c)$.

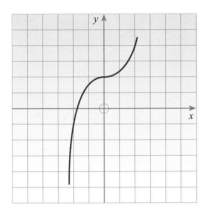

There is one more curve you must know, $y = \frac{1}{x}$, shown below:

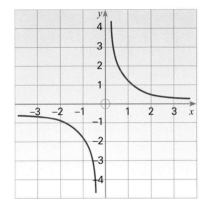

Q What does the graph of $y = x^3 + 4$ look like?

Memorise these curve shapes. You might need to recognise them in the exam.

PRACTICE

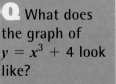

Draw the graphs of the following equations:

1 $y = 2x^3$

2 $y = -2x^3$

3 $y = x^3 + x^2$

4 $y = \frac{x^3}{2}$

5 $y = x^3 + 7x$

6 $y = 2x^3 + 7x$

7 $y = 2x^3 - 5x - 5$

8 $a = b^3 + 2b^2 + 3$

Solving equations with graphs

➤ Well-drawn graphs can provide accurate solutions to some equations and approximate solutions to others.

➤ Algebraic skills, such as expansion of brackets, are vital when solving equations with graphs.

A   Graphs and equations

1 You can use accurately-drawn graphs to find approximate solutions to many equations.

> **KEY FACT**

The solutions of a quadratic equation are the values of x where the curve <u>cuts the x-axis</u>.

2 Draw the graph of $y = x^2 - 9$.

Draw up the table of values.

x	-2	-1	0	1	2
y	-5	-8	-9	-8	-5

Now draw the graph.

> **KEY FACT**

Look at where the curve cuts the x-axis. It cuts at +3 and −3. These are the solutions to the equation.

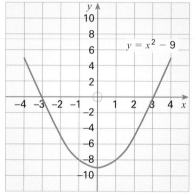

3 Draw a graph of the equation $y = x^2 - 3x - 3$ for values of x from -5 to $+5$, use your graph to solve the equation $x^2 - 3x - 3 = 0$.

Draw up a table of values:

x	-5	-4	-3	-2	-1	0	1	2	3	4	5
y	37	25	15	7	1	-3	-5	-5	-3	1	7

Remember
The solutions to the equation are the values of x, where the curve cuts the x-axis.

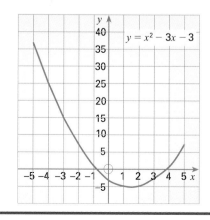

From the graph, you can see that the solutions of the equation are approximately -0.8 and 3.8. Try substituting these values into your equation $x^2 - 3x - 3 = 0$.

Q What is the equation for the line of symmetry of this graph?

B Some examples

Remember
The graph is a parabola.

1 Draw the graph of $y = x^2 - 5x - 3$, use your graph to solve the equation $x^2 - 5x - 3 = 0$.

Draw up the table of values:

x	-3	-2	-1	0	1	2	3	4	5	6	7
x^2	9	4	1	0	1	4	9	16	25	36	49
$-5x$	+15	+10	+5	0	-5	-10	-15	-20	-25	-30	-35
-3	-3	-3	-3	-3	-3	-3	-3	-3	-3	-3	-3
y	21	11	3	-3	-7	-9	-9	-7	-3	3	11

Now draw the graph.
Read off the approximate solutions to the equation $x^2 - 5x - 3 = 0$.

You should find they are approximately -0.6 and 5.6.

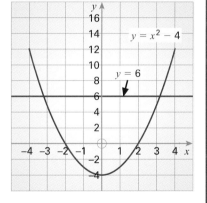

2 Draw the graph of the equation $y = x^2 - 4$ and hence, or otherwise, solve the equation $x^2 - 4 = 6$.

First draw up the table of values:

x	-4	-3	-2	-1	0	1	2	3	4
y	12	5	0	-3	-4	-3	0	5	12

Draw the graph of: $y = x^2 - 4$, then add the graph of $y = 6$.

Look at where the curve and the line cross, read these values off the x axis.
These are the solutions to $x^2 - 4 = 0$.
You can see that the solutions for the equation are approximately $x = 3.2$ or -3.2.

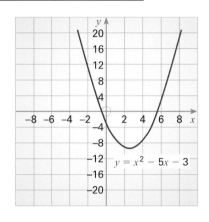

Q Can you remember the special factorisation for $y = x^2 - 4$?

PRACTICE

Draw graphs of the following:

1 $y = (x + 1)(x - 1)$ and use the graph to determine the solution to $x^2 - 1 = 3$.

2 $y = x^2 + 4$ and use the graph to find solutions of $x^2 + 4 = 7$.

3 $y = 2x^2 - 6x$ (use values of x from -1 to $+4$) and use your graph to find solutions to the equation $2x^2 - 6x = 7$.

Trial and improvement

THE BARE BONES

➤ Sometimes you can't find an exact solution to an equation, but can find a reasonable approximation using trial and improvement.

➤ There are two methods you can use: decimal search and bisection.

➤ The accuracy of the approximation depends on the number of trials: the more trials you do, the closer you can get to the solution.

A   Decimal searches

1 Solve the equation $x^2 = 3$, correct to two decimal places.

This is a simple equation which you could solve easily using the square root key! However, it demonstrates the solution process clearly. Notice how the search concentrates on whole numbers, then decimals with one decimal place, then two.

KEY FACT

> **Find the solution one significant figure at a time.**

Record the results of the trials, together with your decisions, in a table like this:

x	x^2	Comments
1	1	Too small, so $x > 1$. Try $x = 2$.
2	4	Too big, so $x < 2$. x is between 1 and 2. Try numbers with one decimal place: try 1.5 first, as it's halfway between 1 and 2.
1.5	2.25	Too small, so $x > 1.5$. Try 1.7, (about halfway between 1.5 and 2).
1.7	2.89	Too small, so $x > 1.7$. Try 1.8.
1.8	3.24	Too big, so $x < 1.8$. x is between 1.7 and 1.8. Move on to numbers with two decimal places. Try 1.75, (between 1.7 and 1.8).
1.75	3.0625	Too big, so $x < 1.75$. Try 1.72 (between 1.7 and 1.75).
1.72	2.9584	Too small, so $x > 1.72$. Try 1.73.
1.73	2.9929	Too small, so $x > 1.73$. Try 1.74.
1.74	3.0276	Too big, so $x < 1.74$. x is between 1.73 and 1.74. You now need to know whether it's closer to 1.73 or 1.74. Trying 1.735 will decide.
1.735	3.010225	Too big, so $x < 1.735$. x is between 1.73 and 1.735.

Q Why was it necessary to try $x = 1.735$, when the answer only needs to be correct to 2 decimal places?

Therefore the solution is $x = 1.73$, to 2 dp.

KEY FACT

> **You try out likely solutions in an equation to see how closely they fit. You use the results to make better guesses.**
> **That's why it's 'trial and improvement', not just 'trial and error'.**

2 Solve the equation $p^3 - 10 = p$, correct to one decimal place.

It's much easier to 'hit the target' with trial and improvement if you're aiming for a fixed number, so rearrange the equation to read $p^3 - p = 10$.

A

p	$p^3 - p$	Comments
1	0	Too small, so $p > 1$. Try $p = 2$.
2	6	Too small, so $p > 2$. Try $p = 3$.
3	24	Too big, so $p < 3$. p is between 2 and 3. Try numbers with one decimal place: try 2.5 first, as it's halfway between 2 and 3.
2.5	13.125	Too big, so $p < 2.5$. Try 2.3, (about halfway between 2 and 2.5).
2.3	9.867	Too small, so $p > 2.3$. Try 2.4.
2.4	11.424	Too big, so $p < 2.4$. p is between 2.3 and 2.4. Is it closer to 2.3 or 2.4? Trying 2.35 will decide.
2.35	10.627875	Too big, so $p < 2.35$. Therefore the solution is $p = 2.3$, to 1 dp.

As you might have guessed, the solution ($p = 2.3089...$) is very close to 2.3!

B *Bisection*

1 In this method, you 'cut' exactly halfway between the previous two guesses.

> Bisection generates accurate solutions quickly but is not 'user-friendly' because the trial numbers need to be carefully calculated and involve lots of decimal places, early on.

EY FACT

2 Solve the equation $x^2 = 3$, correct to two decimal places, using bisection.

x	x^2	Comments
1	1	Too small, so $x > 1$. Try $x = 2$.
2	4	Too big, so $x < 2$. 1.5 is halfway between 1 and 2.
1.5	2.25	Too small, so $x > 1.5$. Try 1.75.
1.75	3.0625	Too big, so $x < 1.75$. Try 1.725.
1.725	2.975625	Too small, so $x > 1.725$. Try 1.7375.
1.7375	3.01890625	Too big, so $x < 1.7375$. Try 1.73125.
1.73125	2.9972265625	Too small, so $x > 1.73125$. Try 1.734375.
1.734375	3.008056640625	Too big, so $x < 1.734375$. x is between 1.73125 and 1.734375.

Q Why was it necessary to go as far as $x = 1.734375$ in the bisection?

Therefore the solution is $x = 1.73$, to 2 dp.

PRACTICE

Use trial and improvement to find solutions to the following equations. Your answers should be to one decimal place.

1 $x^3 - 2x^2 = 1$ **2** $x^3 + 4x - 18 = 0$ **3** $5y^2 - 17y = \frac{7}{4}$

4 $6m^2 - 9 = 6m$ **5** $5t + \frac{3}{2} = 2t^3$

Investigating patterns 1

➤ You must understand how to apply certain thinking skills to solving algebraic problems.

➤ Adopt this strategy: 1) try out some numbers using the rule, 2) draw up a table of results and identify patterns such as first and second differences, 3) construct a rule.

A   Patterns

Remember
Always write the number under each diagram – here it is the numbers of skaters.

1 A group of skaters showed how they made a star pattern.

2 Look at how they built up the star.

- They started by placing one skater at the centre.

- Then a skater joined on each side. This is the pattern:

5

3 Then an extra skater joins on each side.

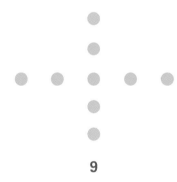

9

4 They continue to build up the pattern by adding a skater on each side.

5 We can build up a table showing the pattern number and the number of skaters.

pattern number (p)	number of skaters (s)	differences
1	1	
		4
2	5	
		4
3	9	
		4
4	13	

Q How many skaters will there be in pattern number 5?

B Finding a rule

1 Look at the 'differences' column in the table at the bottom of page 74.

These are the differences in the number of skaters, so in other words, 4 skaters are added each time. This is important. It tells us that the rule or equation that links the pattern number and the number of skaters is a **linear equation**, because the **differences are all the same**. This means that the equation does not contain powers of p greater than 1.

> Always determine if the relationship is <u>linear</u> first.

2 The differences are constant (4), so multiply the pattern number by 4:

$4 \times 1 = 4, 4 \times 2 = 8$

Does this give the number of skaters? No, multiplying by 4 is not enough. The pattern number (p) $\times$ 4 does not give the number of skaters.

For example, $4 \times 1 = 4$, not 1.

 **What is the rule if the patterns contain 5, 9, 13, 17, . . . skaters?**

3 We need to do something else as well. We need to subtract 3.

4 The rule is: 'pattern number $\times$ 4 $-$ 3 = number of skaters'.

C Writing the rule in algebra

1 In algebra, the rule reads: $4p - 3 = s$

For example:

if $p = 1$ if $p = 2$

$s = 4 \times 1 - 3$ $s = 4 \times 2 - 3$

     $= 4 - 3$ $= 8 - 3$

     $= 1$ $= 5$

The rule has been tested and is correct.

2 Now we can predict the number of skaters for pattern number 5:

$s = 4 \times 5 - 3$

    $= 20 - 3$

    $= 17$

3 Check by drawing. (refer to diagram on right)

 **Check by looking back at the diagrams.**

1 This is a sequence of matchstick triangles.

(a) Continue the sequence.

(b) Build up a table of results and find the rule that connects the number of triangles and the number of matches.

2 This is a sequence of matchstick squares.

(a) Continue the sequence.

(b) Build up a table of results and find a rule that connects the number of squares and the number of matches.

THE BARE BONES

➤ Some relationships are not linear: sometimes you will have to form quadratic equations.

➤ Use the same strategy used for forming linear relationships: 1) try some out, 2) draw up a table of results and identify patterns, 3) find a rule.

A Second differences

1 Here, we have patterns made up of matches:

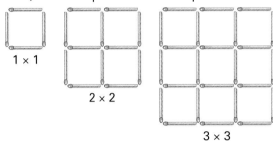

1 × 1

2 × 2

3 × 3

Step 1: make a table of values and look at the differences.

pattern number (n)	number of matches (m)	first differences	second differences
1	4		
		8	
2	12		4
		12	
3	24		4
		16	
4	40		4
		20	
5	60		?
		?	
6	?		

2 We can complete the table by using the differences to predict the number of matches for pattern 6.

Step 2: find the squared term.

Q Why is the first cell in the 2nd difference column blank?

3 As the first differences are not the same, look at the second differences. Here the second differences are all the same, a multiple of two.

This is a clue to the rule for this investigation.

The rule must be a **quadratic**, which means it has a squared term in it.

KEY FACT

The coefficient of n^2 in the formula is half the number in the second difference column.

4 In this case, $4 \div 2 = 2$, so $2n^2$ will be the squared term.

B   Generalising

n	m	n^2	$2n^2$
1	4	1	2
2	12	4	8
3	24	9	18
4	40	16	32
5	60	25	50

1 To find the rule, look at this table.

2 The first line in the table shows that there are 4 matches in pattern 1. If we square the pattern number we get 1. If we then double this number we get 2.

In pattern 2, there are 12 matches.
$$2^2 = 4, 2 \times 4 = 8$$

In pattern 3, there are 24 matches.
$$3^2 = 9, 2 \times 9 = 18$$

3 If you look at the column headed $2n^2$, you will see that we have to add a multiple of 2 to the numbers in this column to get the number of matches.

On the first line, the number in the $2n^2$ column is 2. If we add 2×1 to this, we get 4, the number in the matches column (m).

On the second line, the number in the $2n^2$ column is 8. Add 2×2 and we get 12, the number of matches, and so on.

4 So the rule connecting the number of matches and the diagram number must be $m = 2n^2 + 2n$, where m is the number of matches and n is the pattern number.

5 So for pattern 3, using the rule $m = 2n^2 + 2n$:

$$\text{number of matches} = 2(3)^2 + 6$$
$$= 18 + 6$$
$$= 24 \text{ matches}$$

If you look at the table, you will see that pattern 3 does indeed use 24 matches.

Q How many matches does pattern 10 need?

There are usually some questions like this in the exam. Practice making up tables of differences for investigations and finding the rule.

PRACTICE

For each of these sequences:

a) find the nth-term formula

b) calculate the 20th term.

1 3, 7, 13, 21, 31 . . .

2 1, 8, 19, 34, 53 . . .

3 1, 13, 33, 61, 97 . . .

4 9, 11, 11, 9, 5 . . .

5 1, 3, 6, 10, 15 . . .

THE BARE BONES

➤ Collecting and displaying data are essential tools for mathematicians, scientists and business people.

➤ There is a thinking model for data handling, QCAI: Q = query, C = collect data, A = analyse data (drawing graphs and charts), I = interpretation (saying what the graphs and charts actually mean).

A   What is a pie chart?

> **KEY FACT**

Pie charts are circular diagrams – the shape of a pie – split up to show sectors, or 'slices', that represent each part of the survey. By looking at the size of each sector, it is possible to estimate the fraction of the total for each data item.

1

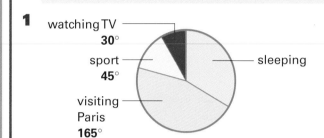

watching TV
30°
sport
45°
sleeping
visiting
Paris
165°

This pie chart shows how a group of students on a school trip in France spent the day and represents a full 24-hour day.

Remember
Here you are interpreting the data, that is saying what it means.

2 They had to travel a long way from their hostel to visit Paris. What fraction of the day was spent sleeping?

To find the answer, you have to work out the angle for the sleeping sector.

A pie chart is a circle and there are 360° in a circle.

Add up the angles for the other sectors.

$30° + 45° + 165° = 240°$

So, the angle for the sleeping sector is: $360° - 240° = 120°$

The fraction for sleeping is $\frac{120°}{360°}$, which cancels to $\frac{1}{3}$.

3 How many hours in the day were spent visiting Paris?

This is shown as 165° on the chart.

To find the answer you first have to work out what 165° is as a fraction of 360°.

$\frac{165°}{360°}$ cancels to $\frac{11}{24}$

To find out how long this is in hours, multiply the fraction by 24 hours giving an answer of 11 hours.

Q Can you draw a pie chart for data you have collected?

Data interpretation allows you to see patterns and trends in data.

B Calculating angles in a pie chart

This data was collected in a survey of 300 people's favourite holiday destinations:

60 Australia   **40 UK**   **150 Spain**   **50 France**

You can see that Spain is the favourite place. It can also be shown on a pie chart. A pie chart has impact because it is **visual**.

KEY FACT

To find the angle at the centre of the sector, calculate:

$\frac{\text{number of people}}{\text{total in survey}} \times 360°$

The results are:

Australia $\frac{60}{300} \times 360° = 72°$ UK $\frac{40}{300} \times 360° = 48°$

Spain $\frac{150}{300} \times 360° = 180°$ France $\frac{50}{300} \times 360° = 60°$

Q Check if the angles add up to 360°.

C Drawing the pie chart

KEY FACT

1: Draw a circle. **2**: Draw in a radius.
3: Measure the angles from this line.

1 This table shows the number of cars in a car park:

type of car	Ford	Toyota	Volvo	Alfa Romeo
number of cars	70	52	35	23

2 Calculate the angles for each sector.

Total number of cars = 70 + 52 + 35 + 23 = 180 cars

180 cars is equivalent to 360°.

Use the unitary method.

So, one car = $\frac{360}{180}$ = 2°.

One car is 2° on the pie chart.

So 70 cars must be 70 × 2° = 140°.

Q Work out the angles for the other cars and draw the pie chart.

PRACTICE

1 This table contains data showing the number of films of each category shown in a city:

classification	18	15	12	PG	U	total
frequency	42	46	56	43	53	

Draw a pie chart to show this information.

2 Draw a pie chart to show the following data:

red balloons 30   yellow balloons 50   green balloons 120   white balloons 100

THE BARE BONES

➤ You can use scatter diagrams to show the relationship between two variables, for example do people with big hands have big feet?

➤ Where there is a link between variables, it is called a correlation.

A Drawing lines of best fit

1 This diagram shows a **correlation cloud**.

Remember
It is easier to draw lines of best fit with a transparent ruler.

strong positive correlation

2 Here, there is a definite link, it is called a **positive correlation**.

KEY FACT

> In the diagram above, the aim is to draw a line through the points so that the points are <u>evenly distributed about the line</u>.

This means that the sum of the distances above the line is roughly equal to the sum of the distances below the line. It may mean that none of the points actually lie on the line.

3 This is called a **line of best fit**.
A line of best fit has two uses:
- to show the correlation more clearly
- to make predictions about other data items.

You might be asked to comment on the nature of the correlation. This means you have to say what type of correlation exists between the variables. Is it positive, negative or is there no correlation?

Q Explain the term 'positive correlation'.

B   *Different types of correlation*

Where the points are scattered closely around the line, there is a <u>strong correlation</u>.

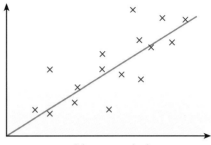

positive correlation

1 If the points are more loosely scattered around the line, there is a moderate correlation. This means that any predictions would be rough estimates, especially if the points are widely scattered, as they are in this diagram.

If the points are so scattered that there is no obvious line, then there is <u>no correlation</u>.

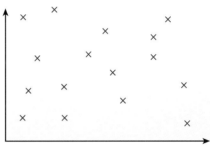

no correlation

2 If the correlation cloud is scattered from top left to bottom right, the correlation is a **negative** correlation. This occurs when, as one quantity increases, the other quantity decreases.

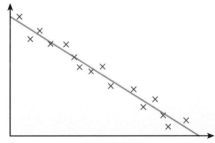

negative correlation

Q What type of correlation exists between height and arm stretch?

PRACTICE

This table shows the heights and weights of 10 people:

height (cm)	150	152	154	158	159	160	165	170	175	181
weight (kg)	57	64	66	66	62	67	75	69	72	76

1 Draw the scatter diagram to represent the data.

2 Comment on the correlation between height and weight.

3 Nisha weighs 58 kg. Estimate her height.

(On one axis, use 2 cm to represent 5 cm of height and start at 145 cm. On the other axis, use 2 cm for 5 kg, starting at 55 kg.)

Finding averages

THE BARE BONES

➤ An average is a single measure that gives an indication of the typical value of a set of data.

➤ There are three main types of average: mode, median and mean.

A The mode

KEY FACT

> The mode is the <u>most common value in a set</u>.

1 This **frequency table** shows the number of pencils that children in one class have in their pencil cases:

number of pencils	0–4	5–9	10–14	15–19	20–24
frequency	8	5	4	12	2

The number of pencils has been placed in groups (e.g. 0–4), so there is some information we don't know. For example, we don't know how many children had eighteen pencils in their pencil case, even though it may be true that more children had eighteen pencils than any other number of pencils.

KEY FACT

> In the case of data in groups or classes, the group with the <u>highest frequency</u> is called the <u>modal group</u>.

2 So, in this example it is not possible to give the mode as a single figure. What is clear is that more children had between 15 and 19 pencils than any other number of pencils. This is called the **modal group**.

3 The mode is used in the clothing industry. Clothes are produced for the size of person that occurs the most, i.e. the average-sized man or woman.

Q What happens if two data items have the same (maximum) frequency?

B The median

KEY FACT

> The median is the <u>middle value in a set</u>, when all the numbers are arranged in order. If you have an even number of data items, the median is the mean of the middle two numbers.

Q Find the median of this set of numbers: 2, 3, 1, 6, 2, 1, 3, 3, 4, 2.

1 The median can also be found by totalling the frequencies.

2 In the table in A, above, the total is 31. Remember the median is the **middle term**, so count up from the left-hand side of the table.

3 The median must be the contents of the pencil case of the sixteenth child and since that child is in the 10–14 group, then the median lies in this group.

C The mean

> The mean is the <u>most frequently-used average</u>.
> It is calculated by taking the sum of all the data items,
> then dividing by the number of items.

Remember
The mean is more correctly called the 'arithmetic mean'.

1 In a frequency table, you multiply the data values by the frequencies.

2 In the example of the table opposite we do not know exactly how many pencils each child has. So it is not possible to calculate the mean accurately.

3 But if we assume that the items in each group are evenly spread, we can use the 'half-way value' to represent the group. To find an approximate to the mean of this data.

Q Find the mean of this set of numbers: 2, 3, 1, 6, 2, 1, 3, 3, 4, 2.

number of pencils	f	mid-point, x	fx
0–4	8	2	16
5–9	5	7	35
10–14	4	12	48
15–19	12	17	204
20–24	2	22	44
total	31		347

4 Therefore, the mean number of items is approximately $347 \div 31 = 11.19$ pencils (to 2 decimal places).

D Continuous data

1 For continuous data the calculation of the mean is carried out in the same way.

2 This table gives the weights of chicks four days after hatching:

weight, w grams	f	mid-point, x	fx
$0 < w \leq 3$	3	1.5	4.5
$3 < w \leq 6$	4	4.5	18
$6 < w \leq 9$	12	7.5	90
$9 < w \leq 12$	6	10.5	63
total	25		175.5

3 Therefore, the mean weight is approximately $175.5 \div 25 = 7.02$ grams.

Q Why are the weight groups not $0 \leq w \leq 3$, $3 \leq w \leq 6$ etc.?

PRACTICE

44 boxes of apples were examined and the number of damaged apples in each box was recorded:

damaged apples	0–4	5–9	10–14	15–19	20–24
frequency	15	10	9	6	4

1 Estimate the mean value for this distribution.

2 What is the modal class for this distribution?

Cumulative frequency

➤ Think of cumulative frequency as a running total. The frequencies are added as you go along.

➤ The median, quartiles and interquartile range can be estimated from the curve.

A Drawing a cumulative frequency diagram

KEY FACT

A cumulative frequency curve often has an S-shape.

1 It is split into a number of parts:

- The **median** is at the 50% point and is known as Q_2.
- The **upper quartile** is at the 75% point and is known as Q_3 or *UQ*.
- The **lower quartile** is at the 25% point and is known as Q_1 or *LQ*.
- The upper and lower quartiles are used to find the central 50% of the distribution. This is known as the **interquartile range**.

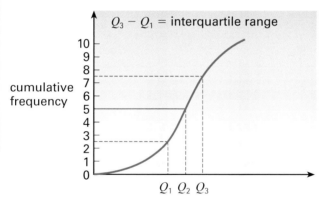

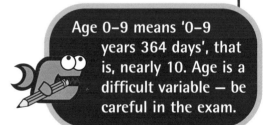

Age 0–9 means '0–9 years 364 days', that is, nearly 10. Age is a difficult variable – be careful in the exam.

2 This table illustrates the **age distribution** in a village of 720 people:

age	0–9	10–19	20–29	30–39	40–49	50–59	60–69	70–79	80–100
frequency	48	72	65	120	153	50	72	96	44

We can draw a cumulative frequency diagram to illustrate this data.

age (less than)	10	20	30	40	50	60	70	80	100
cumulative frequency	48	120	185	305	458	508	580	676	720

The cumulative frequency table is built up by adding the frequencies to what came before, so the 120 in the second cell is 48 + 72 (from the first table).

The 185 in the third cell is the 120 from the second cell + 65 from the first table, and so on.

There is a sketch of how this diagram should look on the opposite page.

Q Can you describe the interquartile range?

B Using the diagram

Remember
The interquartile range is half of the distribution. It is important because it shows how widely the data is spread.

1 This is a sketch of the curve from the information in the table opposite. It has age plotted against **cumulative frequency**.

Q_1, Q_2 and Q_3 go across to the curve and then down to the age-axis. So the value of Q_1 is the value the downward line makes with the age-axis, and not 25%.

2 You could draw your own accurate graph using the information in the tables. You can use this sketch or your graph to find the **median** and the **interquartile range**.

- **Median**:

The median is Q_2, so draw a line from the 50% mark on the cumulative frequency axis, that is half-way through the distribution, across to the curve and then down to the age-axis.

This value is the median.

- **Interquartile range**:

Draw a line from Q_3 and Q_1 across to the curve and then down to the age-axis.

The interquartile range = $Q_3 - Q_1$.

Q_3 on this sketch is 64, Q_1 is 30, so the interquartile range is $64 - 30 = 34$.

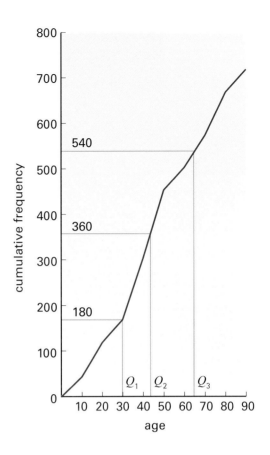

Q Why are the quartiles not 25, 50 and 75 years?

PRACTICE

This is the age distribution of the population of a country:

age	number of people (Millions)
under 10	16
10–19	12
20–29	17
30–39	16
40–49	15
50–69	10
70–89	4

1 Use the information in the table to draw a cumulative frequency table.

2 Use the information in the table to draw the cumulative frequency curve.

3 Estimate the median and interquartile range.

THE BARE BONES

➤ Probability is the mathematics of chance.

➤ An event has a number of possible outcomes. Each outcome has a probability, a number describing the chance that it will happen.

➤ Probabilities are fractions, decimals or percentages measured on a scale from 0 (impossible) to 1 (certain).

A The probability of events

KEY FACT

The probability of something happening doesn't mean it definitely will happen, it simply gives us a measure of the chance of it happening.

Remember
Sometimes the outcomes of an event are equally likely (have the same probability). For many events, they are not.

Q In a bag containing
8 oranges,
5 apples and
4 bananas.
Find the probability that a fruit picked at random is:

(a) an orange
(b) an apple
(c) a banana.

1 If a playing card is picked **at random** from a pack of 52, what is the probability that it is:
(a) a Queen   (b) the Ace of Hearts   (c) a Club?

To answer this, think about the number of cards and the number of chances. There are Hearts, Clubs, Spades and Diamonds in a pack of cards so there must be 4 cards that are printed as Queen cards.

The probability of a Queen must be $\frac{4}{52}$.   Cancel this down to get $\frac{1}{13}$.

There is only one Ace of Hearts, so the probability must be $\frac{1}{52}$.

There are 13 Clubs in a pack of cards, so the probability of picking a Club is $\frac{13}{52}$, which cancels down to $\frac{1}{4}$.

2 A bag contains 6 green balls, 3 yellow balls and 2 red balls. A ball is taken out at random. What is the probability that it is:
(a) a red ball?   (b) a green ball?   (c) a yellow ball?

There are 2 red balls out of a total of 11, so the probability of red $= \frac{2}{11}$.

There are 6 green balls, so the probability of green is $\frac{6}{11}$.

There are 3 yellow balls, so the probability of yellow is $\frac{3}{11}$.

Add up all the probabilities in the answers. You will notice that **all of the probabilities add up to 1**.

B Listing outcomes from events

Q Write down the possible results when three coins are flipped (e.g. all tails = TTT).

1 When a die is rolled and a coin is spun through the air simultaneously, we have two events occurring.
2 The result on the die does not affect the result on the coin – the two events are **independent** of each other.

3 The possible outcomes are:

die	coin	die	coin	
1	h	1	t	h = heads
2	h	2	t	t = tails
3	h	3	t	
4	h	4	t	
5	h	5	t	
6	h	6	t	

C Sample spaces

1 A good way to show outcomes is on a sample space table.

Sample spaces are also known as <u>possibility spaces</u> or <u>probability spaces</u>.

2 The table shows the combinations of the two events. Let's say that throwing an even number and spinning a coin to get a head is a win. The sample space looks like this:

die	h	t
6	win	lose
5	lose	lose
4	win	lose
3	lose	lose
2	win	lose
1	lose	lose

Q Draw a sample space table for rolling two fair dice.

D Relative frequency

1 Relative frequency is a term used to describe the probability of an event, based on results of **trials or experiments**.

> To work out the relative frequency as an estimate of an event occurring, use the following equation:
> **Relative frequency** $= \frac{\text{Number of successful trials}}{\text{Total number of trials}}$

The relative frequency of an event occurring can be used when it is not possible to determine probabilities based on equally likely outcomes.

2 You can perform this experiment and record your results. Spin a coin through the air for 250 spins. Tabulate the results after every 50 spins. Use the formula above to work out the relative frequency. Draw a graph of your results showing relative frequency on one axis and the number of trials on the other axis.

You should find that with the higher number of spins, your results for the number of heads tends to be half the total number of spins.

Q Why don't you get exactly 125 heads and 125 tails?

PRACTICE

1 A bag contains 14 white balls, 12 red balls and 12 yellow balls. After 3 white balls, 4 red balls and 7 yellow balls have been removed, what is the probability that the next ball chosen will be white?

2 'When a fair die is rolled, the probability of getting an even number is not equal to the probability of getting an odd number.' Is this statement true or false? Use a mathematical argument to justify your answer.

3 A 20p coin, a 2p coin and a £1 coin are all spun through the air together. List all the possible orders in which they can land.

4 List all the possible landing orders when a 10 cent coin, a £1 coin, a 10p coin and a £2 coin are spun through the air together.

5 A green spinner with the numbers 1, 2, 3 on it and a blue spinner with the numbers 1, 3, 5 are spun together. List all the possible outcomes.

Mutually exclusive outcomes

THE BARE BONES

➤ If two outcomes are mutually exclusive, it means they cannot happen at the same time.
➤ The probability that something will happen is 1 minus the probability of it not happening.

A Probability

KEY FACT

1 Mutually exclusive outcomes cannot happen at the same time.

- If one outcome occurs, it prevents the other outcome from happening.
- The spin of a coin will give either a head or a tail. Both head and tail cannot appear at the same time, so they are mutually exclusive.

KEY FACT

When the probabilities of mutually exclusive outcomes are added together, the answer is 1.

The probability that something <u>will not happen</u> is: 1 minus the probability of it <u>happening</u>.

Q Use this method to answer the following question. A playing card is selected at random from a pack of 52. What is the probability of not selecting a King?

2 The probability that it will NOT rain tomorrow in Caerleon is $\frac{3}{10}$. What is the probability that it WILL rain tomorrow?

The probability that it will rain in Caerleon tomorrow is 1 minus the probability that it will not rain, that is:

$$1 - \tfrac{3}{10} = \tfrac{7}{10}$$

With a probability this high, it seems likely to rain, so it would be a good idea to take an umbrella in this area!

Make sure you know how to calculate with fractions.

B The 'OR' rule

EY FACT

When two outcomes, X and Y, of an event are mutually exclusive, the probability of one or the other occurring is the sum of their probabilities: P(X OR Y) = P(X) + P(Y).

Remember
You can only use the 'OR' rule if the outcomes are mutually exclusive.

Q Is the probability of selecting a King or a Jack greater than the probability of selecting a King or a Queen in a standard pack of playing cards?

1 A disc is selected at random from a bag containing 5 blue discs, 6 yellow discs and 3 white discs. What is the probability of selecting either a blue disc or a white disc?

The two outcomes are **mutually exclusive**.

P(a blue disc OR a white disc) = P(blue) + P(white)

$$= \frac{5}{14} + \frac{3}{14}$$

$$= \frac{8}{14} = \frac{4}{7}$$

2 A playing card is selected at random from a pack.

What is the probability that it is a Jack or a King?

$$P \text{ (selecting a Jack)} = \frac{4}{52}$$

$$P \text{ (selecting a King)} = \frac{4}{52}$$

$$P \text{ (selecting a Jack OR a King)} = \frac{4}{52} + \frac{4}{52} = \frac{8}{52}$$

$$= \frac{2}{13}$$

PRACTICE

1 The probability of a driver passing her driving test is 0.85. What is the probability of her failing her driving test?

2 When a fair dice is rolled, what is the probability of NOT getting a:

(a) 6   (b) prime number?

3 A bag contains lots of coloured discs. They are white, brown, black and pink. The probabilities of picking each colour of disc are shown in the table:

colour	white	brown	black	pink
probability	0.4	0.3	0.17	

(a) What is the probability of picking a pink disc?

(b) What is the probability of picking a disc that is NOT brown?

4 The probability that I will drive to work tomorrow is 0.95, the probability that I will walk is 0.05.

(a) What is the probability that I will take the bus?

(b) What is the probability that I will drive or walk to work?

5 A bag contains 7 red counters, 8 blue counters and 11 orange counters. One is picked at random.

(a) What is the probability that it is red or blue?

(b) What is the probability that is it not blue?

Independent events

➤ Independent events occur when the outcome of one event does not depend on another event's outcome occurring.

➤ Tree diagrams are a useful way of demonstrating all the possible outcomes from sets of independent events, and their probability.

A The 'AND' rule

Q If you flip a coin, then flip it again, are the results independent?

1 If the occurrence of one event is unaffected by the occurrence of another event, then the events are said to be **independent**. When two events are independent, the probability of one event and the other event occurring is the product of their probabilities.

KEY FACT

This is the 'AND' rule:
P(X AND Y) = P(X) × P(Y)

2 Two coins are spun through the air at the same time. Find the probability of obtaining a head and a head.

P(Head AND Head) = P(H) × P(H)
$= \frac{1}{2} \times \frac{1}{2}$
$= \frac{1}{4}$

3 A coin is spun through the air and a fair dice is rolled. What is the probability of:

(a) obtaining a head on the coin? $= \frac{1}{2}$

(b) obtaining a 6 on the dice? $= \frac{1}{6}$

(c) obtaining a head on the coin AND a 6 on the dice? $= \frac{1}{2} \times \frac{1}{6} = \frac{1}{12}$

B Tree diagrams with two branches

KEY FACT

To read a tree diagram, you need to start at the stem and work along the branches of the tree.

Remember
All the fractions at the end of the pairs of branches should add together to give an answer of 1.

1 A box contains 5 blue discs and 3 red discs. A disc is selected at random and replaced. A second disc is then selected at random. What is the probability that both discs are blue?

To find the probability of a blue followed by a blue, read along the top branch. The probability of a blue and a blue $= \frac{5}{8} \times \frac{5}{8} = \frac{25}{64}$.

2 A box contains 5 blue discs and 3 red discs. A disc is selected at random and NOT replaced. A second disc is then selected at random.

The probability that both discs are blue $= \frac{5}{8} \times \frac{4}{7} = \frac{20}{56} = \frac{5}{14}$.

The probability that one is blue and one is red is the probability of a red and a blue, **or** a blue and a red.

This is an example that uses the AND rule as well as the OR rule. P(a red and a blue) or P(a blue and a red) $= (\frac{3}{8} \times \frac{5}{7}) + (\frac{5}{8} \times \frac{3}{7}) = \frac{15}{28}$.

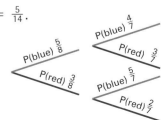

C Tree diagrams with more than 2 branches

1 A bag containing 10 blue balls and 7 white balls is placed on a table.

2 Draw a tree diagram to show all possible combinations for two selections where the balls are replaced after each selection.

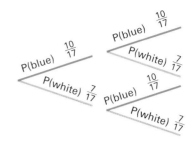

3 What would the tree diagram look like if the process was repeated with 5 extra red balls added to the bag, and if the ball was not replaced after the first selection?

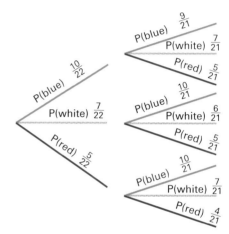

Q What is the probability that you will draw two balls of the same colour?

PRACTICE

1 A card is drawn from a fair pack and a coin is spun through the air. What is the probability that:

(a) it is a black card?

(b) the coin shows tails?

(c) the card is black AND the coin shows tails?

2 A playing card is picked at random from a pack and then replaced. The pack is shuffled before a second card is taken. What is the probability that:

(a) both cards are Clubs?

(b) both cards are Kings?

(c) both cards are not picture cards?

3 A bag contains 5 red counters and 4 blue counters. A counter is drawn at random and replaced before another counter is drawn again. Draw a tree diagram to show all the possible outcomes. What is the possibility that:

(a) two red counters are drawn

(b) a red and a blue counter are drawn.

Number

> There are many specific number questions on both papers, however, many of the facts and skills you learn are used in other branches of mathematics. The questions in this section test 'pure' number skills.

Specimen question 1

In Britain, a television costs £299. In Germany, the same television is sold for €499. The exchange rate is €1 = 61 p on the day we checked.

In which country is the television cheaper, and by how much?

You must show all your working. (3 marks)

Model answer 1

499 × £0.61 = £304.39 | Convert the German price in euros to pounds: 1 mark |

£304.39 – £299.00 = £5.39 | Calculate the difference between the two prices: 1 mark |

The television is cheaper in Britain, by £5.39. | Answer the question: 1 mark |

> - You can only compare the prices if they are in the same currency, so one of them has to be converted.
> - This is a Paper 2 question, and although a calculator was used, you are asked to write the result of each calculation.
> - You could have calculated the difference in euros, because the question doesn't specify which currency to use. To do so, convert £299 to 299 ÷ 0.61 = €490.16.

Specimen question 2

On a TV quiz show, teams buzz to answer a 'starter' question worth 10 points.

- If they interrupt the quizmaster and give a wrong answer, they lose 5 points.
- If they get the starter right, they also answer extra questions worth 5 points each.
- If they get a starter question wrong, but don't interrupt, they score no points.

These were the details of one programme.

	starters correct	starters wrong	starters wrongly interrupted	extra questions
New Bridge College	16	13	5	25
University of Lakeland	18	9	11	26

Who won the game? (3 marks)

Model answer 2

New Bridge College:

$(16 \times 10) + (13 \times 0) - (5 \times 5) + (25 \times 5) = 160 + 0 - 25 + 125 = 260$ points $\boxed{\text{1 mark}}$

University of Lakeland:

$(18 \times 10) + (9 \times 0) - (11 \times 5) + (26 \times 5) = 180 + 0 - 55 + 130 = 255$ points $\boxed{\text{1 mark}}$

New Bridge College won. $\boxed{\text{Answer the question: 1 mark}}$

> • To do this question, calculate the total score for each team.
>
> • This is a Paper 1 question, so the calculations need to be done mentally, or with extra working on the paper. The numbers have been kept easy to help you!
>
> • An alternative (but unorthodox) method is to work out the difference between the teams for each column in the table. This would give Lakeland the following number of points more than New Bridge: $(2 \times 10) + (-4 \times 0) - (6 \times 5) + (1 \times 5) = 20 + 0 - 30 + 5 = -5$ (so Lakeland lost).

Further questions

1 (a) Use your calculator to find $\sqrt{7-1.53}$. Write down all the figures on your calculator.

   (b) Write your answer to 4 significant figures.

2 Which of the following fractions is nearest to $\frac{3}{4}$?

   $\frac{11}{15}$ $\frac{23}{30}$ $\frac{34}{45}$ $\frac{43}{60}$

3 (a) An average human hair is 0.00005 mm in diameter. Write this number in standard index form.

   (b) One of the hairs from Michelle's head is 48 cm long. Assuming it is of average diameter, how many times longer is it than it is wide? Give your answer in standard index form.

4 Find the number exactly halfway between the given numbers.

   (a) 0.41 and 0.44

   (b) −2 and 12

5 Between which two consecutive whole numbers does $\sqrt{72}$ lie?

6 At a dinner, the ratio of vegetarians to non-vegetarians is 4 : 27. There are 216 non-vegetarians. How many vegetarians are there?

Answers to further questions

1 (a) 2.338803113...   (b)   2.339

2 $\frac{3}{4} = \frac{135}{180} = 0.75$

   $\frac{11}{15} = \frac{132}{180} = 0.7333...$

   $\frac{23}{30} = \frac{138}{180} = 0.7666...$

   $\frac{34}{45} = \frac{136}{180} = 0.7555...$

   $\frac{43}{60} = \frac{129}{180} = 0.7166...$

   So $\frac{34}{45}$ is closest.

3 (a) 5×10^{-5} mm

   (b) $480 \div (5 \times 10^{-5}) = 9.6 \times 10^5$ times

4 (a) 0.425

   (b) 5

5 8 and 9

6 $216 \div 27 = 8$; $8 \times 4 = 32$ vegetarians

Shape, space and measures

This part of mathematics covers many different topics, including all work on angles, areas and volumes of shapes, and anything to do with measurement, including speed.

Specimen question 1

(a) Calculate the circumference of a circle of diameter 41 m. State the units of your answer. (2 marks)

(b) Calculate the area of a circle of radius 7 mm. State the units of your answer. (3 marks)

Model answer 1

(a) Circumference = π × diameter | Write down the circle formula |

= π × 41 | Substitute the value for the diameter: 1 mark |

= 128.8052... m | Calculate – write down plenty of digits |

= 128.8 m to 1 dp | Write the answer, rounded to a sensible accuracy: 1 mark |

(b) Area = π × radius² | Write down the circle formula |

= π × 49 | Substitute the value for the radius: 1 mark |

= 153.9380... mm² | Calculate – write down plenty of digits: 1 mark |

= 154 mm² to the nearest square mm | Write the answer, rounded to a sensible accuracy: 1 mark |

- You are expected to know these formulae for the circumference and area of a circle – they are not on the page of formulae.

- Your calculator probably has a π key. Use this to get the greatest accuracy. If you don't have a π key, you will find a value to use (usually 3.142) on the front cover of the paper, or on the page of formulae.

- Use a rough estimate to check the answers to calculations like this: so in (a), use π ≈ 3 and diameter ≈ 40 to get the estimate 3 × 40 = 120 m. This is quite close to the calculated answer.

Specimen question 2

The diagram shows the side of a gardener's cold frame.

(a) Calculate the width (W in the diagram) of the frame. Give your answer to an appropriate degree of accuracy. (4 marks)

(b) Calculate the angle (x in the diagram) that the lid of the frame makes with the horizontal. Give your answer to the nearest degree. (3 marks)

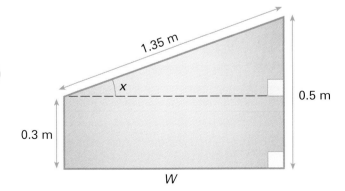

Model answer 2

(a) In the triangle at the top of the diagram, the base is equal to W and the height is 0.5 − 0.3 = 0.2 m.

> You either write this down, draw a diagram like the one below, or mark these lengths on the original diagram: 1 mark

Using Pythagoras' rule, $W^2 = 1.35^2 - 0.2^2$

> State Pythagoras' rule and substitute values: 1 mark

$W^2 = 1.7825$

$W = \sqrt{1.7825}$

> Calculate the square root: 1 mark

$W = 1.335102...$

The width of the frame is 1.335 m, to the nearest millimetre.

> Give the rounded answer: 1 mark

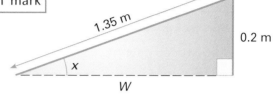

- It is very important to identify the height of the triangle, as you can't get any further without it.
- Remember that you are not finding the hypotenuse in this triangle, so you subtract values in Pythagoras' rule.
- A rounding to the nearest centimetre (1.34 m) would be acceptable. However, nothing less accurate than this will do, because one of the given measurements is already given to the nearest centimetre.

(b) In the triangle, sin x = opposite ÷ hypotenuse

> State the correct trig ratio and...

$= 0.2 \div 1.35$

> ... substitute correctly: 1 mark

$= 0.148148...$

> Calculate sin x

Use the inverse trig ratio to calculate an angle.

So $x = \sin^{-1}(0.148148...)$

$= 8.5196...°$

> Calculate the angle: 1 mark

The lid makes an angle of 9° to the horizontal, to the nearest degree

> Give the rounded answer: 1 mark

- The crucial thing here, of course, is to use the correct trig ratio!
- Remember to keep the value of sin x in calculator memory ready for the inverse sine calculation, so there are no rounding errors.

Further questions

1 **(a)** Draw a co-ordinate grid with x- and y-axes from −2 to 12.

On your grid, draw a trapezium with vertices A(1, 2), B(1, 3), C(3, 5) and D(3, 1).

Calculate the area of trapezium ABCD.

(b) A$_2$(5, 2) and D$_2$(11, −1) are part of an enlargement of ABCD.

Plot A$_2$ and D$_2$ on your grid. What is the scale factor of the enlargement?

(c) Draw the rest of the enlargement. Write down the co-ordinates of B2 and C2.

(d) What are the co-ordinates of the centre of enlargement?

(e) What is the area of the enlargement?

2 The diagram shows the dimensions of a pentagonal prism.

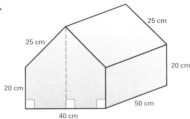

(a) Sketch the net of the prism. Mark on relevant measurements.

(b) Calculate the surface area of the prism.

(c) Calculate the volume of the prism. Give your answer in cubic metres.

Answers to further questions

1 (a) 5 square units

(b) 3

(c) B$_2$(5, 5) and C$_2$(11, 11)

(d) (−1, 2)

(e) 45 square units

2 (a)

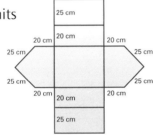

(b) One end $= (40 \times 20) + \frac{1}{2}(40 \times 15)$
$= 1100$ cm^2

Rectangle $= 130 \times 50 = 6500$ cm^2
Total $= 8700$ cm^2

(c) $1100 \times 50 = 55\,000$ cm$^3 = 0.055$ m^3

Algebra

Although algebra includes work on co-ordinates and graphs, the main skill you need is to be able to manipulate and transform algebraic expressions. With this skill, you can solve equations, transform formulae and analyse sequences.

Specimen question 1

Calculate the gradient of the straight line PQ. (2 marks)

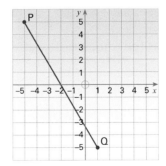

Model answer 1

Gradient = increase in y ÷ increase in x | Write down the fact you are going to use

$= -10 \div 6$ | Substitute values: 1 mark

$= -1.67$ or $-1\frac{2}{3}$ | Calculate the gradient: 1 mark

Two main things can go wrong with a gradient calculation. One is getting the x and y increases mixed up. The other is not using a 'negative increase' when the graph slopes down from left to right.

Specimen question 2

(a)(i) Factorise the expression $x^2 - 3x - 18$ (2 marks)

(ii) Hence solve the equation $x^2 - 3x - 18 = 0$ (1 mark)

(b) Solve the inequality $x^2 < 25$ (2 marks)

Model answer 2

(a)(i) $x^2 - 3x - 18 = (x + ?)(x - ?)$ The two question marks multiply together to make -18, hence the opposite signs: 1 mark

Possibilities are $(x + 1)(x - 18)$ This will give $-17x$

$(x + 2)(x - 9)$ This will give $-7x$

$(x + 3)(x - 6)$ This will give $-3x$: no need to look any further

$(x + 6)(x - 3)$

$(x + 9)(x - 2)$

$(x + 18)(x - 1)$

So $x^2 - 3x - 18 = (x + 3)(x - 6)$ The complete factorisation: 1 mark

- When factorising quadratic expressions, always check that you have the correct sign in each bracket.
- Be sure to make a complete list of the factors of the number term (in this case, -18).

(ii) $x^2 - 3x - 18 = 0$ Write down the equation

So $(x + 3)(x - 6) = 0$ (From part (i))

This is only possible if $(x + 3) = 0$ or $(x - 6) = 0$ If two things multiplied together make 0, one of them must be 0

So $x = -3$ or $x = 6$ The complete solution has two answers: 1 mark

- If the original expression is equal to 0, its factorised version must be too.
- Quadratic equations that can be factorised like this have two solutions. Make sure you give them both.

(b) The equation $x^2 = 25$ has two solutions, $x = 5$ and $x = -5$.   Find the two solutions of the equation: 1 mark

So $x^2 < 25$ could mean that $x < 5$, or $x > -5$.

This can be written as a single inequality, $-5 < x < 5$.   Two separate inequalities would do, but this is neater: 1 mark

Remember that the square root of a positive number has two values: one positive, the other negative.

Specimen question 3

A sequence of numbers begins   2, 7, 12, 17, 22, ...

(a) Find an expression for the nth term of the sequence. (2 marks)

(b) Calculate the 500th term of the sequence. (1 mark)

Model answer 3

(a) Each number in the sequence is 5 more than the last.

This means that the nth term must contain $5n$. | Find the number multiplying n: 1 mark |

If the nth term were $5n$, the first term would be $5 \times 1 = 5$, the second would be 10, and so on.

These terms are always three less than 5, 10, 15...

So the nth term is $5n - 3$. | Find the number added or subtracted from $5n$: 1 mark |

| Remember that if the terms count up in 5s, it doesn't mean that the nth-term expression is $n + 5$! This gives the sequence 6, 7, 8, 9,... |

(b) When $n = 500$, the nth term $= 5n - 3$ | Write down the formula |

$\qquad\qquad = 5 \times 500 - 3$ | Substitute for n |

$\qquad\qquad = 2500 - 3$ | Simplify |

$\qquad\qquad = 2497$ | Calculate the value: 1 mark |

Further questions

1 (a) Expand and simplify $4(3x + 5) - 2(x - 1)$

   (b) Expand and simplify $(3x + 5)(x - 1)$

2 Solve the simultaneous equations:

$5x - 2y = 16$
$3x + 5y = -9$

3 Make d the subject of the formula $S = 4 - 3d$

4 Solve the equation $x^3 - 4x = 10$ by trial and improvement, correct to 1 decimal place.

Answers to further questions

1 (a) $10x + 22$

   (b) $3x^2 + 2x - 5$

2 $x = 2, y = -3$

3 $d = \dfrac{(4 - S)}{3}$

4

x	$x^3 - 4x$	comments
1	-3	$x > 1$
2	0	$x > 2$
3	15	$x < 3$
2.5	5.625	$x > 2.5$
2.6	7.176	$x > 2.6$
2.7	8.883	$x > 2.7$
2.8	10.752	$x < 2.8$
2.75	9.796875	$x > 2.75$

$x = 2.8$ to 1 dp

Data handling covers three main areas: representing data, which involves displaying data in charts and tables, and interpreting it; processing data, which includes work on averages and ranges to describe and compare frequency distributions; and probability, the study of chance events.

Specimen question 1

Here are the first fifty digits of π:

3.14159265358979323846233832795028841197169399375 10

This is a frequency table to show how many times each digit occurs. For example, the digit 6 occurs three times in the first fifty digits.

Digit	0	1	2	3	4	5	6	7	8	9
Frequency	2	6	5	9	3	5	3	4	5	8

A digit is chosen at random. What is the probability the digit will be prime? (3 marks)

Model answer 1

The prime digits are 2, 3, 5 and 7.

> Show the examiners you know what the prime numbers are by writing them down or marking them on the table: 1 mark

The total frequency of the primes = 5 + 9 + 5 + 4 = 23. | Add the frequencies: 1 mark

The probability is $\frac{23}{50}$. | Write the fraction: 1 mark

> This is a Paper 1 question. It is fine to leave the fraction just as it is, although you would be expected to cancel down if possible.

Specimen question 2

The mean height of five trees is 35.6 m.

(a) Find the total of the trees' heights. (2 marks)

One of the trees is rotten and has to be cut down. This changes the mean height of the remaining trees to 39.1 m.

(b) Calculate the height of the tree that was cut down. (2 marks)

Model answer 2

(a) $35.6 \times 5 = 178$ m. | Mean = total ÷ 5, so reverse the calculation: 2 marks. 1 mark is for assembling the correct calculation.

(b) New total = $39.1 \times 4 = 156.4$ m. | Similar calculation to part (a): 1 mark

$178 - 156.4 = 21.6$ m | The difference between the two totals gives the answer: 1 mark

> A wrong answer from part (a) would be followed through.

Specimen question 3

In a trial of a new exam, a group of pupils were asked to finish the paper in 2 hours, but were given extra time if they needed it. This table shows the results.

Time Taken (t)	Frequency (f)
1 hour ≤ t < 1 hour 30 min	3
1 hour 30 min ≤ t < 1 hour 40 min	8
1 hour 40 min ≤ t < 1 hour 50 min	15
1 hour 50 min ≤ t < 2 hours	42
2 hours ≤ t < 2 hours 10 min	83
2 hours 10 min ≤ t < 2 hours 30 min	49

No pupils took less than 1 hour or longer than $2\frac{1}{2}$ hours.

(a) Construct a cumulative frequency table for this data. (2 marks)

(b) Using your table, draw a cumulative frequency graph. (3 marks)

(c) Using your graph, estimate:

    (i) the median time (1 mark)

    (ii) the interquartile range. (2 marks)

Model answer 3

(a)

Time taken (t)	Cumulative Frequency
t < 1 h 30 min	3
t < 1 h 50 min	26
t < 2 h	68
t < 2 h 10 min	151
t < 2 h 30 min	200

2 marks

(b)

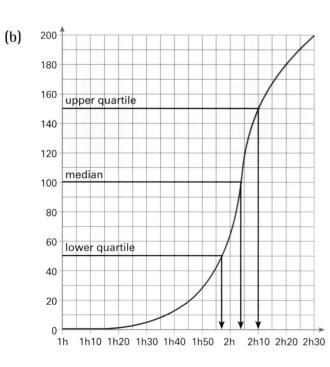

3 marks.
Wrong answers from part (a) would be followed through.

(c) Median = 2h 4 min (1 mark)

Interquartile range = 2h 10min − 1h 57min = 13 min (2 marks)

There will be slight variations on the answers given, depending on the quality of your curve-drawing.

Further questions

1 The following table gives the speed of cars passing a radar checkpoint.

Speed (s km/h)	Frequency (f)
0 ≤ s < 40	6
40 ≤ s < 60	8
60 ≤ s < 70	26
70 ≤ s < 80	82
80 ≤ s < 100	103
100 ≤ s < 150	48

(a) Which is the modal speed class?

(b) How many cars' speeds were recorded altogether?

(c) In which class is the median speed?

(d) Calculate an estimate of the mean speed of the cars. Give your answer to the nearest km/h.

2 In a game at a charity stall, you pay 20p to spin these two fair spinners:

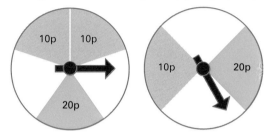

(a) Draw a possibility space diagram to show the possible outcomes.

(b) If the stall made 500 spins in a day, how much money would people have paid to play altogether?

(c) About how many times would you expect each amount to have been paid out in winnings?

(d) How much prize money would have been paid out?

(e) Would the stall make a profit? If so, how much?

Answers to further questions

1 (a) 80 ≤ s ≤ 100   (b) 273   (c) 80 ≤ s < 100

(d)

speed (s km/h)	frequency (f)	mid-interval values (m)	mf
0 ≤ s < 40	6	20	120
40 ≤ s < 60	8	50	400
60 ≤ s < 70	26	65	1690
70 ≤ s < 80	82	75	6150
80 ≤ s < 100	103	90	9270
100 ≤ s < 150	48	125	6000
totals	273	–	23 630

Estimated mean = 23 630 ÷ 273 = 86.55677... km/h = 87 km/h to nearest km/h.

2 (a)

		1st spinner				
		0p	0p	10p	10p	20p
2nd	0p	0p	0p	10p	10p	20p
spinner	0p	0p	0p	10p	10p	20p
	10p	10p	10p	20p	20p	30p
	20p	20p	20p	30p	30p	40p

(b) £100

(c) nothing: 100 times
10p: 150 times
20p: 150 times
30p: 75 times
40p: 25 times

(d) 150 × 10p + 150 × 20p + 75 × 30p + 25 × 40p
= £15 + £30 + £22.50 + £10 = £77.50.

(e) Yes, about £22.50 per 500 goes.

Topic checker

- Go through these questions after you've revised a group of topics, putting a tick if you know the answer, a cross if you don't.
- Try the questions again the next time you revise . . . until you've got a column that's all ticks! Then you'll know you can be confident . . .

Number

1	Work out the equivalent fractions: (a) $\frac{1}{6} = \frac{}{18}$ (b) $\frac{3}{4} = \frac{15}{}$	☐☐☐
2	Change these improper fractions to mixed numbers: (a) $\frac{21}{4}$ (b) $\frac{83}{9}$ (c) $\frac{61}{10}$	☐☐☐
3	Change these mixed numbers to improper fractions: (a) $5\frac{1}{3}$ (b) $22\frac{3}{4}$ (c) $13\frac{1}{8}$	☐☐☐
4	What is the denominator of a fraction?	☐☐☐
5	What is the numerator of a fraction?	☐☐☐
6	Write 60 000 in standard form.	☐☐☐
7	What is 0.000000000075 in standard form?	☐☐☐
8	Change 4.6×10^3 into ordinary form.	☐☐☐
9	Given $\sqrt{R} = \sqrt{\frac{V}{I}}$, find R, when $V = 3.9 \times 10^2$ and $I = 1.32 \times 10^2$.	☐☐☐
10	What is a prime factor?	☐☐☐
11	Express 100 as a product of its prime factors.	☐☐☐
12	What is the next cube number after 27?	☐☐☐

Answers

1 (a) $\frac{1}{6} = \frac{3}{18}$ (b) $\frac{3}{4} = \frac{15}{20}$
2 (a) $\frac{21}{4} = 5\frac{1}{4}$ (b) $\frac{83}{9} = 9\frac{2}{9}$ (c) $\frac{61}{10} = 6\frac{1}{10}$
3 (a) $5\frac{1}{3} = \frac{16}{3}$ (b) $22\frac{3}{4} = \frac{91}{4}$ (c) $13\frac{1}{8} = \frac{105}{8}$
4 The lower part of the fraction.
5 The upper part of the fraction.

6 6×10^4
7 7.5×10^{-11}
8 1.72
9 2.95
10 A factor of a number that is itself a prime.
11 $2^2 \times 5^2$
12 64

13 Write down the first ten terms of the Fibonacci sequence.

14 What are the factors of 100?

15 What is a prime number?

16 Express $\dfrac{t^6}{t^2}$ as a single power of t.

17 Evaluate $16^{\frac{1}{2}}$.

18 Evaluate 15^0.

19 Work out $(y^5)^2$.

20 Calculate $36^{\frac{1}{2}} \div 9^{\frac{1}{2}}$.

21 A school roll of 800 students increased by 15% between September and Christmas. It then increased further by another 5%. How many students are now on the roll?

22 Simplify $\sqrt{12}$ without using a calculator.

23 Find the area of this triangle.

7cm

24cm

24 Find the volume of a triangular prism of length 10 cm, and triangle base length of 3 cm. The prism is 4 cm in height.

25 Find the volume of a cylinder of base radius 15 cm and height 14 cm.

26 What is a sector of a circle?

27 Find the area of a circle with a diameter of 25 cm.

28 A circle has an area of 100 cm^2. Find its radius.

29 What is the circumference of a circle with a diameter of 50 cm?

30 A circle has a circumference of 24 cm, what is its radius?

31 Find the angles in this triangle.

$2x$

$3x$ x

Answers

13 1, 1, 2, 3, 5, 8, 13, 21, 34, 55
14 1, 2, 4, 5, 10, 20, 25, 50, 100
15 A number that has only two factors and the factors are different. The factors are 1 and the number itself.
16 t^4

17 4
18 1
19 y^{10}
20 2
21 966 students
22 $2\sqrt{3}$
23 84 cm^2
24 60 cm^3

25 9896 cm^3
26 A slice, like a slice of a circular pie.
27 490.87 cm^2
28 5.64 cm
29 157.1 cm
30 3.82 cm
31 $x = 30°$, $2x = 60°$, $3x = 90°$

32 What is Pythagoras' rule?

33 Calculate x.

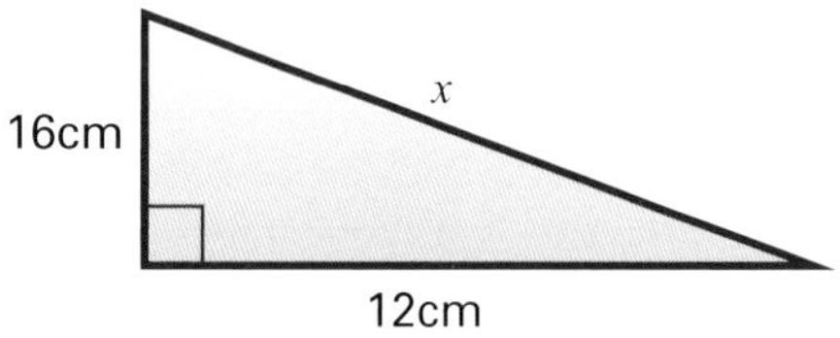

16cm

x

12cm

34 Find the length of *m*.

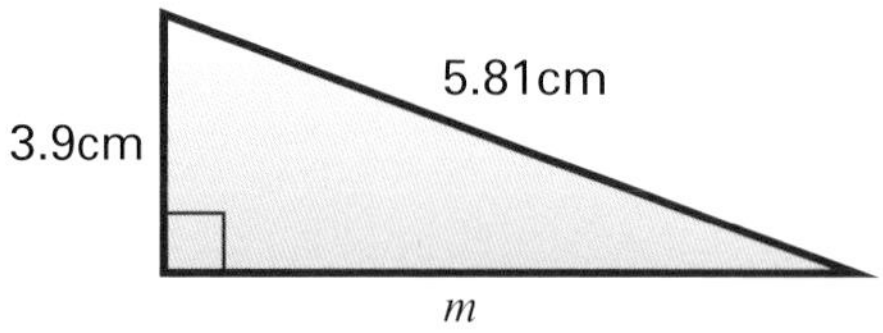

5.81cm

3.9cm

m

35 A square has diagonals of 30 cm, find the length of one of the sides.

36 Find the length of the diagonal of a rectangle that measures 10 cm by 40 cm.

37 A 6m ladder rests against a wall, with its base 1m away from the wall.
How far up the wall does the ladder reach?

38 A plane flies 40km due North and then 60km due East.
How far away is it from its starting point?

39 What is the sine ratio in a right-angled triangle?

40 What is the cosine ratio in a right-angled triangle?

41 What is the tangent ratio in a right-angled triangle?

42 Find x.

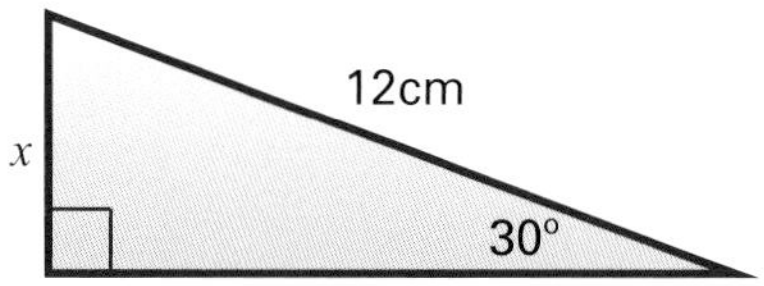

12cm

x

30°

43 Find y.

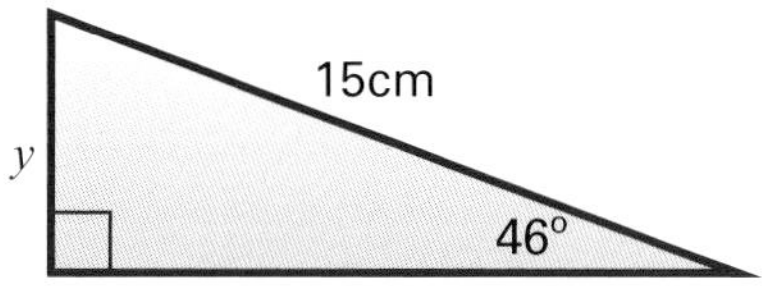

15cm

y

46°

Answers

32 $h^2 = a^2 + b^2$. More formally it is 'the square of the hypotenuse of a right-angled triangle is equal to the sum of the squares of the other two sides'.

33 $x = 20$ cm

34 $m = 4.31$ cm to 2 d.p.

35 21.21 cm to 2 d.p.

36 41.23 cm

37 5.92 m

38 72.11 km

39 $\sin \theta = \frac{O}{H}$

40 $\cos \theta = \frac{A}{H}$

41 $\tan \theta = \frac{O}{A}$

42 $x = 6$

43 $y = 10.8$ cm

Algebra

44 Solve $3x + 5 = 26$.

45 Solve $10 - \frac{1}{4}k = 9$.

46 Solve $5 - 8p = 5p - 21$.

47 Solve $5 - 8y = 37$.

48 Make x the subject of $\frac{p}{x} = m$.

49 Make x the subject of $6 - fx = 4x + j$.

50 Make x the subject of $\frac{ax}{b} = c$.

51 Make c the subject of $E = mc^2$.

52 Solve this inequality $5x - 4 > 6$.

53 Solve this inequality $-9f < 81$.

54 Write down the gradient and y-intercept of the lines described by the following equations:
(a) $y = 9x + 3$ (b) $y = 4 - 3x$ (c) $y = 6x + 5$ (d) $y = 5 - 7x$.

55 Rearrange these equations to make y the subject of the equation and then write down the gradient and the y-intercept: (a) $2x + 3y = 4$ (b) $5x - 7y = 12$.

56 What can you say about the gradient of this line?

57 A line passes through the points (1, 2) and (4, 5). What is the gradient of the line?

58 Find the equation of the line that passes through the point (0, 5) that is parallel to the line $y = 2x + 1$.

59 Solve these simultaneous equations:
$3m + n = 13$ $m - n = -1$

Answers

44 $x = 7$

45 $k = 4$

46 $p = 2$

47 $y = -4$

48 $x = \frac{p}{m}$

49 $x = \frac{6 - j}{f + 4}$

50 $x = \frac{cb}{a}$

51 $c = \sqrt{\frac{E}{m}}$

52 $x > 2$

53 $f > -9$

54 (a) gradient = 9, y-intercept = 3 (b) gradient = -3, y-intercept = 4 (c) gradient = 6, y-intercept = 5 (d) gradient = -7, y-intercept = 5

55 (a) $y = \frac{4 - 2x}{3}$ gradient = $\frac{-2}{3}$ y-intercept = $\frac{4}{3}$

(b) $y = \frac{5x - 12}{7}$ gradient = $\frac{5}{7}$ y-intercept = $-1\frac{5}{7}$

56 It is negative.

57 1

58 $y = 2x + 5$

59 $m = 3$, $n = 4$

60 Solve these simultaneous equations:
$p + 3q = 26 \qquad 2p - q = 3$

61 Solve $3(x + 5) = 42$.

62 Factorise: (a) $100v^2 + 20vc$ (b) $169g^2 - 225h^2$.

63 Expand and simplify: (a) $(x + 3)(x + 5)$ (b) $4x(x + 5)(x + 6)$.

64 Expand and simplify $(x - a)^2$.

65 Draw a diagram to show the regions that satisfy the inequality.
$x + y > 1$.

66 What is an identity?

67 Find the first four terms of these sequences: (a) $u_n = 3n + 2$ (b) $u_n = 5^n$.

68 Find formulae for u_n to describe each of these sequences:
(a) 2, 5, 8, 11 (b) 7, 12, 17, 22.

69 $S = \frac{1}{2}at^2$ Find t, when $s = 90$ and $a = 5$.

70 $m = \sqrt{\frac{d}{2\pi}}$ Find d, when $m = 100$.

71 $A = \pi r^2$ When $A = 169$, find r.

72 Draw the graph of $y = x^2 - 5x + 4$.

73 Draw the graph of $y = x^3 - x^2 + 1$.

74 Draw the graph of $y = x^2 + 1$ and use the graph to solve $x^2 + 1 = 3$.

75 By trial and improvement, find a solution to $z^3 - 10z = 1$, correct to 1 d.p.

Answers

60 $p = 5, q = 7$

61 $x = 9$

62 (a) $20v(5v + c)$ (b) $(13g + 15h)(13g - 15h)$

63 (a) $x^2 + 8x + 15$ (b) $4x^3 + 44x^2 + 120x$

64 $x^2 - 2ax + a^2$

65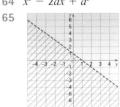

66 A statement that is true for all values of the variables involved in it, eg $2x = x + x$

67 (a) 5, 8, 11, 14 (b) 5, 25, 125, 625

68 (a) $u_n = 3n - 1$ (b) $u_n = 5n + 2$

69 $t = 6$

70 62831.86

71 7.33

72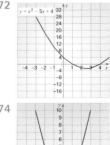

73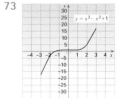

74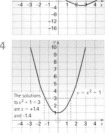
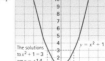
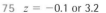

75 $z = -0.1$ or 3.2

Data handling

76 The following data for the number of cars in a car park was collected:

Type of car	Ford	Volvo	Skoda	Toyota
Number of cars	55	25	15	80

Draw a clearly labelled pie chart to show this information. ☐ ☐ ☐

77 What is correlation? ☐ ☐ ☐

78 If the points are scattered closely around the line of best fit on a scatter diagram, what does that say about the correlation? ☐ ☐ ☐

79 If the points are scattered very loosely so that there is no clear line of best fit on a scatter diagram, what does that say about the correlation? ☐ ☐ ☐

80 If the correlation cloud is scattered from top left to bottom right on a scatter diagram, what does that say about the correlation? ☐ ☐ ☐

81 Define these terms exactly: (a) mean (b) median (c) mode (d) range (e) interquartile range. ☐ ☐ ☐

82 What is the result of $Q_3 - Q_1$? ☐ ☐ ☐

Probability

83 What is the 'AND' rule in probability? ☐ ☐ ☐

84 What is the 'OR' rule in probability? ☐ ☐ ☐

85 What are mutually exclusive outcomes? ☐ ☐ ☐

86 What are independent events? ☐ ☐ ☐

87 The red cards in a pack are removed. One card is picked at random. What is the probability of it being: (a) the Ace of Spades (b) a Club (c) not a Diamond (d) the King of Hearts? ☐ ☐ ☐

Answers

76 The pie chart should be divided up:
Ford (113°), Volvo (51°), Skoda (31°),
Toyota (165°).

77 Correlation is a relationship between two sets of data. The classic example is smoking. There is a close correlation between the numbers of people who smoke and those who later develop lung cancer.

78 There is a strong correlation.

79 There is no correlation.

80 It is a negative correlation.

81 (a) The mean is the arithmetical mean. To find the mean, add up all of the data and divide this answer by the number of data items.
(b) The median is the middle number when the data is placed in order of size.

(c) The mode is the item of data that occurs the most often.
(d) The range is the difference between the highest and the lowest values in a data set.
(e) The interquartile range is where the middle 50% of a set of data is located.

82 The interquartile range.

83 Multiply

84 Add

85 Two outcomes of an event, which cannot both occur at once.

86 These are events whose outcomes are not dependent on each other. An example is the weekly lottery of winning balls. The fact that some of the numbers may have appeared last week is totally irrelevant to their chance of appearing this week.

87 (a) $\frac{1}{26}$ (b) $\frac{1}{2}$ (c) 1 (d) 0

Complete the facts

- Fill in the gaps as you revise to test your understanding.
- You could photocopy these pages if you wanted to do this more than once.
- You'll also end up with a concise set of notes on some of the most important ideas.

Fractions and percentages

1   The top and bottom part of a fraction are called _____

2   A percentage is a _____

3   A mixed number is _____

4   When £200 is decreased by 40%, the answer is _____

5   20% of £50 is _____

6   £40 out of £200 is _____%

Standard form

1   $6 \times 10^3 = $ _____

2   When 0.000000000073 is written in standard form, the answer is _____

3   When 4.6×10^5 is changed to a decimal number, the answer is _____

4   When 543 is written in standard form, the answer is _____

5   When 3.45×10^4 is written as a decimal number, the answer is _____

Primes, factors and sequences

1   A prime number is defined as _____

2   The cube number before 125 is _____

3   The Fibonacci sequence starts with 1 and the first eight terms are _____

4   The factors of 21 are _____

5   The factors of 6 contain two numbers that are themselves prime, these numbers are _____

Indices

1   $x^0 = $ _____

2   $m^5 \div m^2 = $ _____

3   $25^{\frac{1}{2}} = $ _____

4   $(x^2)^3 = $ _____

5   $64^{\frac{1}{2}} \div 16^{\frac{1}{2}} = $ _____

Shape

1 The formula for the area of a triangle with base b and height h is _____

2 A prism is_____

3 To calculate the volume of a triangular prism of length 12 cm and triangle base length 10 mm, with a height of 50 mm, we have to _____

_____

4 The volume of a cylinder with radius r and height h is found by using the formula

_____

5 Density is defined as _____

Circles

1 The formula for the area of a circle of radius r is _____

2 The formulae for the circumference of a circle of radius r and diameter d are_____

3 The area of a circle of radius 4 cm is _____

4 The circumference of a circle of diameter 14 cm is _____

5 A circle with an area of 120 cm² has a radius of _____

Angles and triangle

1 An angle less than 90° belongs to the set of angles that are called_____ angles.

2 An angle greater than 90° but less than 180° is an _____ angle.

3 An angle greater than 180° is a _____angle.

4 Allied angles add up to _____

5 Alternate angles on a transversal between parallel lines are _____

Pythagoras' rule

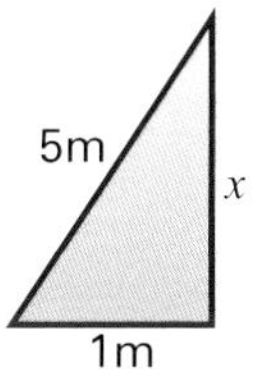

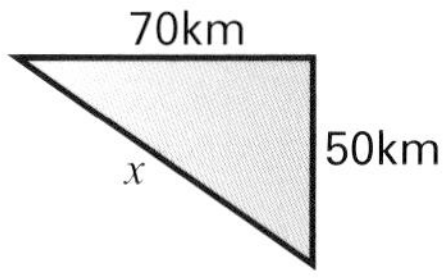

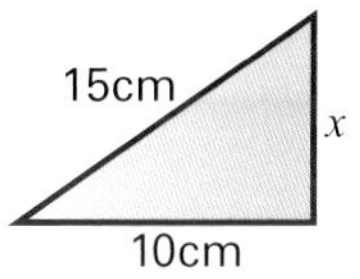

1 Algebraically, Pythagoras' rule is written as _____

2 When a diagonal is drawn across a square, it is possible to calculate its length by using
Pythagoras. For instance, when calculating the diagonal of a square of side length 6 cm,
the calculation is _____

3 This diagram shows a ladder of 5 m length, leaning against a wall. The base of the ladder is 1m away from the base of the wall. To find out how far up the wall the ladder reaches, we need to:

_____

_____

4 A fishing trawler sails 50 km due North to fishing grounds. Then it travels to new fishing grounds 70 km due West. To find its distance from the starting point, we need to_____

5 Examiners often label the slant height on a cone and ask students to work out the surface area. For instance, when we have a cone with base radius of 10cm and slant height 15 cm, the perpendicular height is _____

Trigonometry

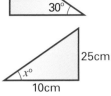

1   The sine of 30^0 is written as _____

2   The cosine of 45^0 = _____

3   The tangent of 45^0 = _____

4   To find the length of x, we need to use trigonometry _____

_____

5   To find the size of angle x, we need to _____

_____

Algebra

1   To solve the equation $4x + 9 = 41$, the steps are _____

_____

2   To solve $20 - \frac{1}{4}j = 15$, the calculation is _____

3   To solve $6p - 5 = 121 - 8p$, the calculation is _____

4   To make x the subject of $8 - fx = 7x + p$, the calculation is _____

5   To make x the subject of $\frac{xy}{z} = a$ the calculation is_____

6   To make C the subject of $F = HC^2$ the calculation is_____

7   To solve the inequality $6x - 6 < 36$, the calculation is_____

8   The gradient and y-intercept of the graph of the equation $y = 2x - 3$ are_____

9   When a line passes through two points, say (1,3) and (2,5), to work out the gradient of the line we

_____

10   To find the equation of the line that passes through the point (0,4) and that is parallel to the line
$y = 2x + 2$, we _____

11   The solutions to the simultaneous equations:
$5t + 6u = 57$ $t + u = 10$ are _____

12   The solutions to the simultaneous equations:
$a + 3b = 26$ $2a - b = 3$ are _____

13   To solve the equation $8(d + 9) = 128$, the calculation is _____

14   When $100h^2 + 25hx$ is factorised, the calculation is _____

15   When $196k^2 - 225m^2$ is factorised, the calculation is _____

16   When $(x + 5)(x + 9)$ is expanded, the calculation is _____

17   When $(x - b)^2$ is expanded, the calculation is _____

18   The first four terms of the sequence $u_n = 2x + 1$ are _____

19   The first three terms of the sequence $u_n = 5y - 1$ are _____

20   A good example of the use of algebra in other areas of mathematics, is in the calculation of the
circumference of a circle. For instance, to find the circumference of a circle of radius 15cm, the
calculation is _____

_____

21 We can use the method of trial and improvement to find the solution to certain equations. For instance, to find the solution of $x^3 + 2x^2 + 3x + 5 = 17\frac{3}{8}$, the calculation is _____

_____

22 When $v^2 = u^2 + 2as$, we can find v, when $u = 10$, $a = 12$ and $s = 15$ by _____

Data handling

1 Correlation is _____

2 A loose correlation can be seen when _____

3 When the points in a correlation cloud are scattered from top left to bottom right, it means _____

_____

4 The mean of a set of data is _____

5 The median of a set of data is_____

6 The problem of finding the median is slightly harder when there is an even number of data items. Here the procedure is to _____

7 The interquartile range is an important measure because _____

8 The range is defined as _____

9 The mode is also known as the modal class in a grouped frequency distribution. This is defined as____

_____

Probability

1 The AND rule in probability is an indication that we need to _____

2 The OR rule in probability is an indication that we need to _____

3 The probability of not picking the Ace of Hearts from a fair pack of cards is _____

4 Mutually exclusive outcomes cannot _____

5 When a fair die is rolled and then rolled again, the probability of getting a 1 and then a 6 in that order is_____

6 The probability of not rolling a 6 on a fair die is _____

7 The probability of selecting a card from a fair pack and getting a red card is _____

8 Given a bag of discs, where there are 8 white, and 3 red discs, the probability of picking a white and then a red, where the first disc is not replaced, is _____

9 Given a bag of discs, where there are 8 white, and 3 red discs, the probability of picking a white and then a red, where the first disc is replaced, is_____

10 Relative frequency is defined as _____

11 Rolling a die and spinning a coin through the air are examples of events where the outcome of one is not dependent on the outcome of the other. These are known as _____

12 The probability that the sun will rise tomorrow is 1. This is because the event of the sun rising somewhere on the Earth is_____

13 The probability that you can grow a third leg is 0. This is because this event is _____

14 When two dice are rolled, and the numbers are added together, the probability of getting a 7 is the highest of all the probabilities. This is because _____

Answers

Fractions and percentages

1. numerator and denominator
2. fraction over 100
3. whole number and a fraction
4. £120   5 £10   6 20%

Standard form

1. 6000
2. 7.3×10^{-11} 3 460000
3. 5.43×10^2 5 34500

Primes, factors and sequences

1. A number that has only two factors that are different (1 and the number itself).
2. 64
3. 1, 1, 2, 3, 5, 8, 13, 21
4. 1, 3, 7, 21
5. 2 and 5

Indices

1. 1   2 m^3
3. 5   4 x^6 5 2

Shape

1. $A = \frac{1}{2}bh$
2. a solid, uniform cross-section
3. Convert all measurements to same units; calculate the area of the triangular cross-section; multiply the area by the length of the prism.
4. $V = \pi r^2 h$
5. ratio of mass to volume

Circles

1. $A = \pi r^2$
2. $C = 2\pi r$ and $C = \pi d$
3. 50.27 cm^2
4. 43.98 cm
5. 6.18 cm

Angles and triangles

1. acute   2 obtuse 3 reflex
4. 180°   5 equal

Pythagoras' rule

1. $h^2 = a^2 + b^2$
2. $x^2 = 6^2 + 6^2$

$x^2 = 36 + 36 = 72$

$x = 8.48$cm

3. Use Pythagoras:

$5^2 - 1^2 = x^2$

$x = \sqrt{24} = 4.9$ m

4. $x^2 = 70^2 + 50^2$

$= 4900 + 2500$

$x = 86$ km (to nearest km)

5. Use Pythagoras:

$15^2 - 10^2 = x^2$

$x = 11.18$ cm

Trigonometry

1. $\sin 30° = \frac{1}{2}$ 2 0.707106781
3. 1
4. $\sin 30° = \frac{x}{30}$

$x = 30 \sin 30°$

$x = 15$

5. $\tan x = \frac{25}{10}$

$\tan x = 2.5$

$\tan^{-1} 2.5 = 68.20$

Algebra

1. Subtract 9 from both sides, then divide both sides by 4
2. $20 - \frac{1}{4}j + \frac{1}{4}j = 15 + \frac{1}{4}j$

$20 - 15 = \frac{1}{4}j$

$\frac{1}{4}j = 5$

$j = 20$

3. $6p - 5 + 5 = 121 - 8p + 5$

$6p = 126 - 8p$

$6p + 8p = 126$

$14p = 126$

$p = 9$

4. $8 - fx + fx = 7x + p + fx$

$8 - p = 7x + fx$

factorise the right-hand side:

$8 - p = x(7 - f)$

divide both sides by $(7 - f)$:

$x = \dfrac{8 - p}{7 - f}$

5. multiply both sides by z:

$\dfrac{xyz}{z} = az$

the zs on the left-hand side cancel out: $xy = az$

divide both sides by y:

$\dfrac{xy}{y} = \dfrac{az}{y}$

The ys on the left-hand side cancel out. So the answer is:

$x = \dfrac{az}{y}$

6. divide both sides by H:

$\dfrac{F}{H} = \dfrac{HC^2}{H}$

Hs cancel on right-hand side:

$\dfrac{F}{H} = C^2$

to get C, take the square root of both sides:

$C = \sqrt{\dfrac{F}{H}}$

7. $6x - 6 + 6 < 36 + 6$

$6x < 42$

$x < 7$

8. gradient = 2 y-intercept = -3

9. Use the fact that the gradient is the increase in the y values divided by the increase in the x values. If we call the gradient m, then the calculation is:

$m = \dfrac{y - y_1}{x - x_1}$ $m = \dfrac{5 - 3}{2 - 1}$

$m = 2$, the line's gradient is 2.

10. Use the facts in the question. We know the line passes through (0,4). As this must be on the y-axis, it must be the y-intercept (where the line cuts the y-axis). This also tells us that the end of the equation is +4, because the equation will be of the general form $y = mx + c$, where m is the gradient of the line and c is the y-intercept. We have therefore established that the y-intercept is +4. We also know that the line we require is parallel to the line $y = 2x + 2$. If it is parallel, it must be equal in gradient to the known line $y = 2x + 2$. Since we know the gradient of this line is 2, then the gradient of the other line must be 2. Therefore:

$y = 2x + 4$
11 $5t + 6u = 57$ (i)
   $t + u = 10$ (ii)
Multiply equation (ii) by 5:
$5t + 5u = 50$ (iii)
We now have:
$5t + 5u = 50$ (iii)
$5t + 6u = 57$ (i)
Equation (i) − equation (iii):
$u = 7$
Now substitute for u in (i):
$5t + 42 = 57$
$5t = 15$
$t = 3$
Sub for t and u in equation
(ii): $3 + 7 = 10$
12 $a + 3b = 26$ (i)
   $2a − b = 3$ (ii)
Multiply equation (i) by 2:
$2a + 6b = 52$ (iii)
$2a − b = 3$ (ii)
Equation (iii) − equation (ii):
$7b = 49$
$b = 7$
Substitute for b into (ii):
$2a − 7 = 3$
$2a = 10$
$a = 5$
Substitute for a and b into (ii):
$10 − 7 = 3$
13 $8d + 72 = 128$
   $8d = 56$
   $d = 7$
14 $25h(4h + x)$
15 $(14k − 15m)(14k + 15m)$
16 $= x^2 + 9x + 5x + 45$
   $= x^2 + 14x + 45$
17 $(x − b)^2 = (x − b)(x − b)$
   $= x^2 − xb − xb + b^2$
   $= x^2 − 2xb + b^2$
18 3, 5, 7, 9
19 4, 9, 14
20 $C = 2\pi r$
   $C = 2 \times \pi \times 15$
   $C = 94.25$ cm
21

a	b	c	c replaces (a+b) ÷2
0	2	1	*
1	2	1.5	solution

So this shows us the solution
of the equation is $x = 1.5$
22 $v^2 = u^2 + 2as$
   $v^2 = 100 + (2 \times 12 \times 15)$
   $v^2 = 460$
   $v = 21.45$

Data handling

1 A relationship that exists between two sets of data. E.g. the direct relationship between height and length of leg – most tall people have long legs. Occasionally you will find a tall person who has a long trunk and shorter legs, but that does not deny the fact that there is a relationship between height and the length of leg, that relationship is called a correlation.
2 The points on a scatter-graph are loosely gathered around the line of best fit.
3 The correlation is negative.
4 The arithmetical average. The items of data are added and then the answer is divided by the number of items.
5 The middle number when the data is order of size, from lowest to highest or highest to lowest.
6 Find the mean of the middle two items of data. For instance, if the data were 1, 2, 3, 4, then there is no middle term and therefore no apparent median. So we take the middle two terms, 3 and 4, add them together and divide by 2. This gives us the mean of these two items of data and the median of the whole set of data. Here it is the case that the median is not part of the original set of data.
7 It is a measure of the spread of the middle 50% of the distribution.
8 The highest value item of data minus the lowest value item of data.
9 The item of data that occurs the most frequently. The most common example of this is the average-sized man or woman. This has implications for the clothing industry.

Probability

1 Multiply the probabilities.
2 Add the probabilities.
3 $\frac{51}{52}$
4 Both happen at the same time.
5 $\frac{1}{36}$
6 $\frac{5}{6}$
7 $\frac{1}{2}$
8 $\frac{12}{55}$
9 $\frac{24}{121}$
10 Probability that is based on previous experience.
11 Independent events
12 A certainty
13 An impossibility
14 There are more ways of making 7 from the numbers on the two dice than any other number from 2 to 12. So 7 has more chances of occurring when the dice are rolled. This means it is the most likely and therefore has the highest probability.

Money, time and distance

1 320   2 4 and 9

3 £40.80   4 £5.80

5 £1, 20p, 5p, 2p   6 16:15 hrs

7 30 hours and 5 minutes

Working with fractions

1 (a) $\frac{3}{6}$ (b) $\frac{9}{12}$

2 (a) $3\frac{3}{4}$ (b) $3\frac{1}{7}$ (c) $10\frac{1}{5}$ (d) $9\frac{1}{9}$

3 (a) $\frac{13}{3}$ (b) $\frac{97}{8}$ (c) $\frac{88}{9}$ (d) $\frac{111}{4}$

Working with indices

1 (a) 3   (b) $\frac{1}{3}$ (c) 27

2 (a) 1   (b) 5^{-6}, 0.000064

  (c) 6   (d) $\frac{1}{8}$

3 8

4 1

5 1

Numbers and standard form

1 6×10^2 (b) 2×10^6

(c) 4.1×10^4 (d) 9.55×10^5

(e) 9×10^{-4} (f) 3×10^{-3}

(g) 1.01×10^{-6} (h) 5.8×10^{-1}

2 8000   (b) 400 000

(c) 2 100 000 000   (d) 70 030 000

(e) 0.3   (f) 0.00000005

(g) 0.0575   (h) 0.00000677

Standard form: calculations

1 2.65×10^{52} 2 (a) 6×10^{17} (b) 6.67×10^6

3 1.333×10^9 4 1.369×10^{-11}

5 1.5×10^{-1}

Sequences

1 (a) 1, 2, 4, 5, 8, 10, 20, 40

  (b) 1, 2, 4, 5, 10, 20, 25, 50, 100   (c) 1, 5, 17, 85

2 (a) $2^3 \times 3^2 \times 5$ (b) 2×11 (c) $2 \times 3^2 \times 5$

3 31, 37, 41, 43, 47   4 121, 144

5 64, 125   6 10, 15, 21, 28

7 20 and 40   8 4, 20 and 100

9 30, 60 and 90

Ratio, proportion and percentages

1 (a) 1:125   (b) 1:8

2 (a) 56.45 Euros   (b) 229.03 Euros

  (c) 2419.35 Euros

3 4500   4 $6\frac{2}{3}$ m   5 £63

Surds

1 (a) $2\sqrt{6}$ (b) $2\sqrt{7}$ (c) 0   (d) 2

2 (a) $5\sqrt{3}$ (b) $-3\sqrt{3}$ (c) $6\sqrt{3}$ (d) $2\sqrt{3} + 4\sqrt{2}$ (e) $2\sqrt{2}$

Measuring and rounding

1 (a) 1 m   (b) 30 feet   (c) 12 cm   (d) 0.25 cm

2 (a) 1 m   (b) 294 cm (most people would probably
                             round this to 3 m)

3 About 26 pounds   4 approx $45\frac{1}{2}$ mph   5 333 kg/m³

Dimensions

1 (a) $2\pi r$ length   (b) πr^2 area

  (c) $\pi r^2 h$ volume   (d) $2\pi rh$ area

2 There are too many dimensions. For it to be area, it must have only 2 dimensions.

3 It must represent a volume since it is of dimension three.

Calculating the area of shapes

1 17.5 m²   2 206 m²   3 3 rolls

4 7 tins   5 22.75 cm²   6 10 cm

Finding the volume

1 60 m³   2 108 m³

3 3770 cm³   4 0.62 m³

5 78 m³   6 49763 cm³ (49800 cm³)

Circles 1

1 (a) 43.98 cm   (b) 12.57 cm   (c) 78.54 cm   (d) 68.49 cm

2 (a) 50.27 cm²   (b) 452.39 cm²

3 (a) 15.90 m²   (b) 21.49 m²

4 5.64 cm

Circles 2

1 $a = 84°$ 2 $x = 50°$, $y = 45°$, $z = 95°$

3 $x = 85°$, $y = 95°$, $z = 85°$

Angles and triangles

1 $x = 28°$ 2 $x = 30°$, $2x = 60°$, $3x = 90°$

3 $a = 97°$ (3rd angle in a triangle)

  $b = 83°$ (allied angle to a)

  $c = 97°$ (corresponding to a)

  $d = 129°$ (allied angle to 51°)

  $e = 51°$ (corresponding angle to 51°)

4 $x = 45°$, $y = 45°$, $z = 135°$

Pythagoras' rule

1 10.01 cm (2 dp)   2 23.82 cm (2 dp)

3 10.63 cm (2 dp)   4 13.23 cm (2 dp)

Solving problems – Pythagoras' rule

1 4.58 m (to 2 dp)   2 50 km

3 30 km   4 Prakash ($15^2 = 12^2 + 9^2$)

5 2.97 m (2 dp)   6 (a) 9.9 (b) 8.1 (c) 5.4

Sines, cosines and tangents

1 (a) 0.258819045   (b) 0.669130606

  (c) 1.482560969

2 (a) $31°$ (30.99) (b) $55°$

(c) $42°$ (41.99°)

3 6.88 cm   4 10.4 cm   5 29.11m

6 (a) $62.18°$ (b) $30°$ (c) $47.3°$ (d) $58.4°$

Solving simple equations

1 $x = 7$ 2 $y = 9$ 3 $d = 2$ 4 $f = 12$

5 $c = 5$ 6 $h = \frac{1}{2}$ 7 $x = 3$ 8 $x = -1$

9 $k = 6$ 10 $p = \frac{2}{3}$

Rearranging formulae

1 $x = r - 9$ 2 $x = a + z$

3 $x = \frac{16 - 4y}{5}$ 4 $x = \sqrt{\frac{c}{m}}$

5 $x = 4m$ 6 $x = p^2 + pc$

7 $x = \frac{cb}{m}$ 8 $x = \frac{5-p}{3+f}$

9 $y = \frac{9 - 2x}{5}$ 10 $y = \frac{x}{2} - 5$

Inequalities

1 $x \leqslant 5$ 2 $x > -3\frac{1}{2}$ 3 $a \geqslant \frac{1}{6}$

4 $t \geqslant -1\frac{1}{3}$ 5 $d > -5$ 6 $w \leqslant -2\frac{1}{2}$

7 $f \geqslant -8$ 8 $\frac{3}{2} > p > \frac{1}{2}$ 9 $-\frac{1}{5} \leqslant r \leqslant 2$

10 $-15 < t < 9$

Lines and equations

1 gradient $= 7$, y-intercept $= 3$

2 gradient $= 3$, y-intercept $= -5$

3 gradient $= \frac{1}{3}$, y-intercept $= 12$

4 gradient $= 3$, y-intercept $= -2$

5 gradient $= -3$, y-intercept $= 4$

6 gradient $= 2$, y-intercept $= -7$

7 $y = 4x + 5$ 8 $y = x + 6$ 9 $y = 2x + 1$

Simultaneous linear equations

1 $x = 3, y = 7$

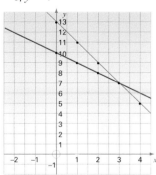

2 6 days

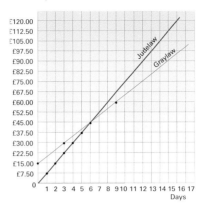

3a 300 booklets

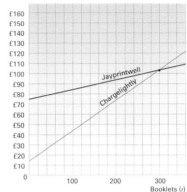

3b £105

Simultaneous equations and algebra

1 (a) $x = 5, y = 2$ (b) $a = 7, b = 4$

(c) $m = 9, n = 1$ (d) $t = 6, r = 7$

(e) $x = 5, y = 4$ (f) $c = 7, d = 9$

(g) $e = 12, f = 7$ (h) $p = 15, q = -2$

(i) $a = 2, b = 1$ (j) $p = 4, q = 2$

2 $a = 60, b = 8$

3 (a) $a = -\frac{2}{3}$ $b = -\frac{8}{9}$ (b) $m = \frac{3}{4}$

Using brackets in algebra

1 $x = 4$ 2 $x = 10$

3 $x = -8$ 4 $x = 4.5$

5 $x = -5\frac{1}{3}$ 6 $x = 4$

7 $x = 15\frac{1}{2}$

8 (a) $7x(2x + 1)$ (b) $9y(4y - 1)$

9 (a) $5y^2(3y^2 + 5)$ (b) $20a(5a + b^3)$

Multiplying bracketed expressions

1 $x^2 + 4x + 3$ 2 $x^2 + 9x + 14$

3 $x^2 + 4x + 4$ 4 $x^2 + nx + mx + mn$

5 $x^2 + 6x + 8$ 6 $x^2 - 2ax + a^2$

7 $x^2 - 6x + 9$ 8 $a^2 - 2ax + x^2$

9 $x^2 - 2xy + y^2$ 10 $x^2 - 4$

11 $x^2 - 9y^2$ 12 $36 - x^2$

Regions

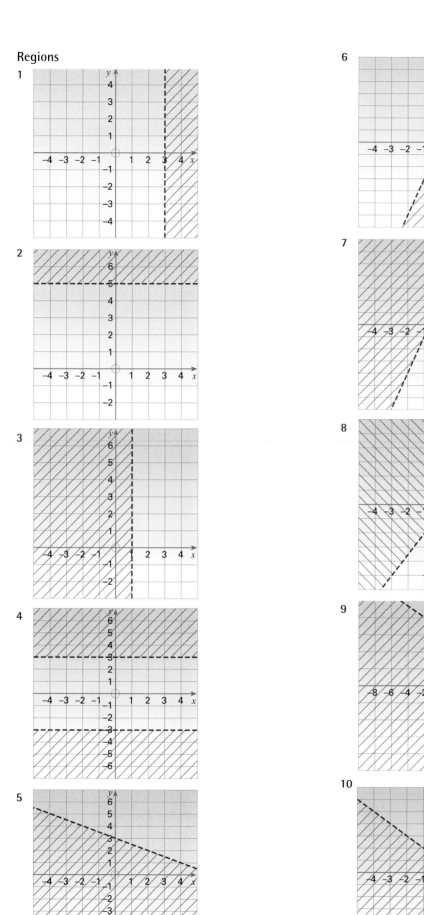

Sequences and formulae

1 (a) $u_1 = 3$, $u_2 = 6$, $u_3 = 9$, $u_4 = 12$
  (b) 3, 5, 7, 9　　　　(c) −3, 1, 5, 9
  (d) 15, 13, 11, 9　　(e) 3, 9, 27, 81
  (f) 1, $\frac{4}{3}$, $\frac{3}{2}$, $\frac{8}{5}$

2 (a) $n = 7$　(b) $n = 7$　(c) $n = 9$

3 (a) $5n - 3$　(b) $5n + 1$　(c) $8n + 1$　(d) $3n - 1$

More on formulae

1 22　　　　　　2 196.07 cm^2　　3 29.22 cm

4 1960.36　　　5 5026.55　　　　6 6.95

7 4.47　　　　　8 6.41

Quadratic equations

1
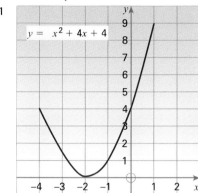

2
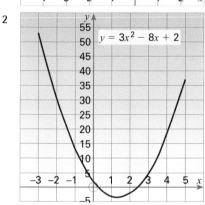

3 The graph meets the y-axis at the origin.
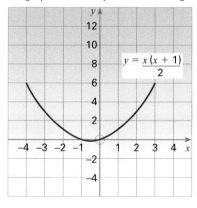

Cubic and reciprocal functions

1
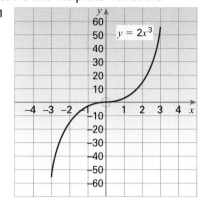

2
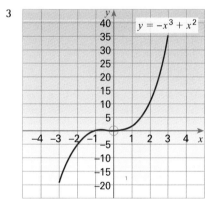

3
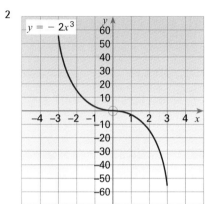

4
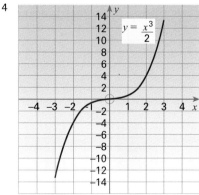

5

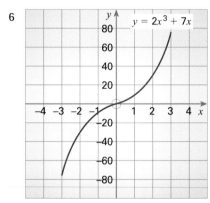

$y = x^3 + 7x$

6

$y = 2x^3 + 7x$

7

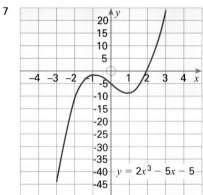

$y = 2x^3 - 5x - 5$

8

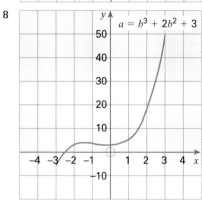

$a = b^3 + 2b^2 + 3$

Solving equations with graphs

1 Solutions are $x = +2$ or $x = -2$

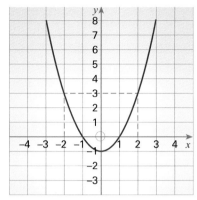

2 Solutions are $x = +1.7$ or -1.7

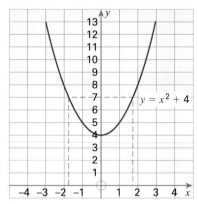

$y = x^2 + 4$

3 Solutions are $x = $ approx -1.9 or $+3.9$

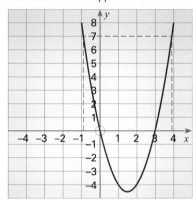

Trial and improvement

1 1.5   2 2.1   3 3.5
4 1.8   5 1.7

Investigating patterns 1

1 $2n + 1 = t$ (where n = number of matches and t = number of triangles)

2 $3n + 1 = s$ (where n = number of matches and s = number of squares)

Investigating patterns 2

1 $u_n = n^2 + n + 1$; $u_{20} = 421$
2 $u_n = 2n^2 + n - 2$; $u_{20} = 818$

3 $u_n = 4n^2 - 3$; $u_{20} = 1597$
4 $u_n = -n^2 + 5n + 5$; $u_{20} = -295$
5 $u_n = \frac{1}{2}n^2 + \frac{1}{2}n$; $u_{20} = 210$

Pie charts

1   2

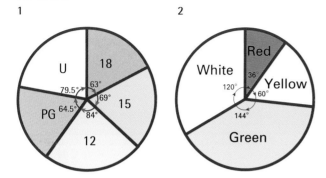

Scatter diagrams and correlation

1

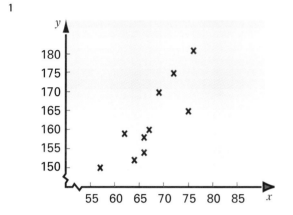

2 There is a strong correlation between height and weight.
3 Nisha's height will be about 152 cm.

Finding averages

1 Mean value 9 apples (8.95)
2 Modal class is 0–4.

Cumulative frequency

1

Age	No of people (Millions)	Cumulative freq
under 10	16	16
10-19	12	28
20-29	17	45
30-39	16	61
40-49	15	76
49-69	10	86
69-89	4	90

2

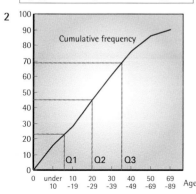

3 (approximately) median = 30; IQR = 43 − 15 = 28

Probability

1 $\frac{11}{24}$ 2 False, $P(\text{even}) = \frac{1}{2}$ $P(\text{odd}) = \frac{1}{2}$

3
20p	2p	£1
20p	£1	2p
£1	20p	2p
£1	2p	20p
2p	£1	20p
2p	20p	£1

4
10 cents	£1	10p	£2
10 cents	£1	£2	10p
10 cents	£2	£1	10p
10 cents	£2	10p	£1
10 cents	10p	£2	£1
10 cents	10p	£1	£2
£1	10 cents	10p	£2
£1	10 cents	£2	10p
£1	£2	10 cents	10p
£1	£2	10p	10 cents
£1	10p	£2	10 cents
£1	10p	10 cents	£2
10p	10 cents	£1	£2
10p	10 cents	£2	£1
10p	£2	10 cents	£1
10p	£2	£1	10 cents
10p	£1	£2	10 cents
10p	£1	10 cents	£2
£2	10 cents	£1	10p
£2	10 cents	10p	£1
£2	10p	£1	10 cents
£2	£1	10 cents	£1
£2	£1	10 cents	10p
£2	£1	10p	10 cents

5
G1B1	G1B3	G1B5
G2B1	G2B3	G2B5
G3B1	G3B3	G3B5

Mutually exclusive outcomes

1 0.15   2 (a) $\frac{5}{6}$ (b) $\frac{1}{2}$

3 (a) 0.13   (b) 0.7

4 (a) 0   (b) 1

5 (a) $\frac{15}{26}$ (b) $\frac{9}{13}$

Independent events

1 (a) $\frac{1}{2}$ (b) $\frac{1}{2}$ (c) $\frac{1}{4}$

2 (a) $\frac{1}{16}$ (b) $\frac{1}{169}$ (c) $\frac{100}{169}$

3 (a) $\frac{25}{81}$ (b) $\frac{20}{8}$

Answers to check questions

Money, time and distance

Nineteenth century.

Because they are redundant cells. The distance from Bristol to Bristol doesn't exist.

Working with fractions

$\frac{75}{100}$, $\frac{15}{20}$, $\frac{6}{8}$, $\frac{9}{12}$, $\frac{12}{16}$

$\frac{1}{3}$

$\frac{4}{12} + \frac{3}{12} = \frac{7}{12}$

4

Working with indices 1

2^9 (512)

7^5 (16807)

$(4^3)^3 = 4^9$

$\frac{1}{32}$

$\sqrt[4]{x}$

Numbers in standard form

The number before the multiplication sign isn't between 1 and 10.

The number is 388×10^6, but this isn't standard form.

Yes. Add 1 to the number of zeros, then make the result negative. That gives the index.

2 000 000 000 000 (two trillion)

Standard form: calculations

9.7×10^8

0.002

try 2^{332}, then 2^{333}

Square (when on a single key), square root, trig functions, reciprocal etc.

Sequences

$100 = 2 \times 2 \times 5 \times 5$

$\quad\ = 2^2 \times 5^2$

Squares: 1, 4, 9, 16, 25, 36, 49, 64, 81, 100, 121, 144, 169, 196

Cubes: 1, 8, 27, 64, 125

15

Add the last two terms to get the next.

28

Ratio, proportion and percentages

Any number (e.g. 2 : 3 : 6 : 1)

At £1 = 63p, £50 = €79.36

0.85, 1.3, 0.6

Surds

Anything minus itself is zero.

The two sides are equal.

Measuring and rounding

$\text{time} = \frac{\text{distance}}{\text{speed}}$

Dimensions

It is a length.

It is a sum of two areas.

Because it only has two dimensions and a volume must have three.

Calculating the area of shapes

115.5 cm^2

A triangle is half a parallelogram

Finding the volume

Divided both sides by 176.71.

$V = \frac{1}{2}bhl$

volume = $6 \times 6 \times 6 = 216$ cm^3

Circles 1

Yes.

56.5 cm to 1 d.p.

Halve the diameter to get the radius.

Angles and triangles

$180 - 48$ gives the sum of the two angles, so this has to be halved.

scalene

Pythagoras' rule

Use the sides of the triangle for the bases of three squares – the areas of the squares obey the rule.

No, $9^2 + 12^2 = 225$ and $16^2 = 256$.

11.2 cm

Both $\sqrt{50} = 7.1$ cm to 1 d.p.

Solving problems – Pythagoras' rule

10.8 cm to 1 d.p.

$15^2 = x^2 + x^2$

$x = 10.6$ cm

Sines, cosines and tangents

All $40°$ right-angled triangles are mathematically similar to one another, so the opposite and adjacent sides are always in the same ratio.

$\cos x = \frac{A}{H}$ or $\tan x = \frac{O}{A}$

The calculator returns an error. No angle has a sine of 1.5.

Solving simple equations

The number multiplying x.

$y = 4; k = \frac{2}{9}; n = -1\frac{1}{3}; r = \frac{1}{2}$

Rearranging formulae

$x = p - y$

$p/6 - q/6$

$d = u + v$

$n = W/[t - s]$

Inequalities

minus three is less than x, which is less than or equal to $+6$.

We divided by 4 because it is the coefficient of x.

Lines and equations

They have the same coefficient of x.

Infinite.

$\frac{1}{2} \times 4 + 2 = 4$

The equation has the same coefficient of x as the known line, but the same y intercept as c.

Simultaneous linear equations

They cross at (5, 11)

Paying £600 and then £30 monthly.

Solving simultaneous equations

$25 + 16 + 18 - 14 = 41 + 4$.

Check that $45 = 45$

Multiplying equation (ii) by 3 to give $3x + 3y = 36$

Because it created a simpler equation.

Multiply equation (i) by 2 and (ii) by 3 then subtract.

Using brackets in algebra

$15x^3$

$5xy$

$x = 6$

$5 \times (-6) = -30$

Multiplying bracketed expressions

$2wy + 2wz + xy + xz$

$x \times (-x) = -x^2$

$x^2 + 10x + 25$

$x^2 - 49$

Regions

$x < 4$

$2 \leqslant x \leqslant 4$ and $-1 \leqslant y \leqslant 5$

Because $y = 1$ is included in the inequality.

Sequences and formulae

$u_3 = 2 \times 3 + 1 = 7$

$u_{100} = 5 \times 100 + 4 = 504$

$u_n = 5n - 1$

They are not equivalent, for example, they are not equal when $x = 1$.

More on formulae

$x = 2.86$ to 2 d.p.

Subtract 5 from both sides, then swap sides so that t is on the left-hand side.

Quadratic functions

The y-axis.

Graphing cubic and reciprocal functions

$3x$ means $3 \times x$

x^3 means $x \times x \times x$

The same as $y = x^3$, translated 4 units in the y direction.

Solving equations with graphs

$x = 1\frac{1}{2}$

$y = (x - 2)(x + 2)$

Trial and improvement

Because you cannot be sure how much more than 1.73 it is and it may affect the rounding.

Because you cannot be sure how much more than 1.734375 it is and it may affect the rounding.

Investigating patterns 1

17

$\times 4 + 1$ instead of $\times 4 - 3$

Investigating patterns 2

You need at least 3 terms of the sequence to generate a second difference.

220

Scatter diagrams and correlation

When something is directly affected by the other factor. E.g. age and height.

Strongly positive.

Finding averages

They are both modes of the data.

2.5

2.7

You wouldn't know which group to put 3 g, 6 g or 9 g in.

Cumulative frequency

It contains the middle 50% of the data.

You find the 25%, 50% and 75% marks on the cumulative frequency axis and work across to the age axis.

Probability

0.471, 0.294, 0.235

Probability only forecasts results approximately.

Mutually exclusive outcomes

$1 - \frac{1}{13} = \frac{12}{13}$

They are both the same.

Independent events

Yes. The result of the first flip does not affect the second.

$\frac{15}{77} + \frac{1}{11} + \frac{10}{231} = \frac{76}{231} = 0.33$

Glossary

A

Acute angle An angle less than 90° (less than a right angle).

Algebra The branch of mathematics that deals with the general case. Algebra involves the use of letters to represent variables and is a very powerful tool in problem-solving.

Angle A measure of space between two intersecting lines.

Arc Part of the circumference of a circle.

Area A measure of two-dimensional space.

Average See mean, median and mode.

B

Bar chart A frequency chart, where the frequency of the data is proportional to the height of the bar.

Bearing A measure of an angle used in navigation.

C

Chord A line across a circle, not passing through the centre.

Circumference The complete boundary of a circle.

Coefficient The number in front of the variable that shows the magnitude (size) of the variable, for example in $2x$ the coefficient of x is 2 and in $5y$ the coefficient of y is 5.

Compound interest The type of interest that is paid by most banks, where the interest is added to the principle invested and then in subsequent years interest is earned by the original interest.

Correlation The relationship between two variables. It can be a positive correlation; in other words, as one of the variables increases, the other increases in the same proportion. Alternatively, it could be a negative correlation, where as one of the variables increases, the other decreases in the same proportion. An example is smoking. There is a positive correlation between smoking and lung cancer and other diseases. You may be unfortunate and get lung cancer without ever smoking but a high number of lung cancer sufferers are also smokers. The more you smoke, the more you increase your chances of becoming ill.

Cube A three-dimensional solid which has sides of equal length.

Cube root The cube root of a number, for example 64, is the number that you need to multiply by itself and then by itself again to make, in this case, 64. Mathematically, this must be 4, because $4 \times 4 = 16$ and then $16 \times 4 = 64$. We write this as $\sqrt[3]{64}$

and this reads as 'the cube root of 64'.

Cumulative frequency Think of this as a running total graph. Add up the frequencies as you go through the data. The cumulative frequency is drawn as a typical 'S' shaped graph. The curve is also known as an ogive.

Cylinder A three-dimensional solid with a uniform cross-section that is a circle.

D

Denominator The lower part of a fraction.

Diameter The distance across a circle from one point on the circumference to another point on the circumference, passing through the centre.

Dimension A dimension is a length. Formulae can be analysed to determine what type of formulae they may be. For example, $A = lb$, where l and b are both lengths, could be an area. This is because a formula for area must contain two lengths. A formula for volume must contain three lengths.

Distribution A set of data.

Dodecahedron A regular solid with 12 faces.

E

Equation A mathematical statement, usually in algebra, where two sides of the statement are equal. The aim is to work out the value of the unknown by manipulating the equation.

Equation, linear An equation where the highest power of any of the terms is 1.

Equation, quadratic An equation where the highest power of any of the terms is 2.

Equilateral triangle A triangle that has all three sides of equal length and all three angles equal 60°.

Estimate The process of comparing the size of a property of an object with a known quantity.

Euro Europe-wide currency that was established in 1999 and introduced into many European countries in 2002.

F

Factor A number or variable that divides into other numbers or variables without a remainder.

Factorisation The process of extracting the highest common factors from an expression.

Formula An algebraic statement that is the result of previously established work. A formula is accepted to be correct and can be used in subsequent work. For example, $A = \pi r^2$ is accepted as the formula for the area of a circle. It is not necessary to prove this formula every time we need to use it.

Frequency polygon A way of displaying grouped data where the mid-values of the class intervals are joined by lines.

Function A rule which applies to one set of quantities and how they relate to another set.

Generalising A process in mathematical thinking, where a general rule, usually expressed in algebra, is determined.

Gradient The measurement of the steepness of a line. It is the ratio of the vertical to the horizontal distance. Where a line slopes from bottom left to top right, the gradient is positive. Where the line slopes from top left to bottom right, the gradient is negative.

Graph A visual display, used to show information from data distributions, to create a visual understanding of the nature of the distribution.

Graphical calculator An electronic calculator on which it is possible to draw graphs.

Highest common factor The highest factor that will divide exactly into two or more numbers.

Hypotenuse The longest side of a right-angled triangle.

Identity An algebraic expression where the two sides of the identity are equal because they are not different, for example
$2x = x + x$.

Imperial units The traditional units of measure which were once used in the UK and the USA, such as feet, inches, pints and gallons.

Improper fraction A fraction where the numerator is of a higher value than the denominator.

Independent event An event whose outcome is not dependent on the outcomes of other events.

Inequality An algebraic statement which is unequal.

Integer A whole number.

Interquartile range The spread of the middle 50% of a distribution.

Irrational number A number that cannot be totally determined, for example √2.

Isosceles triangle A triangle with two equal sides and two equal angles, and where the equal sides are opposite the equal angles.

Line of symmetry A line that bisects a shape so that each part of the shape reflects the other.

Lowest common multiple The lowest number that two or more numbers will go into, for example the lowest common multiple of 4 and 8 is 8, because 8 is the lowest number that both 4 and 8 will go into.

Mean The arithmetic average, which is calculated by adding all of the items of data and then by dividing the answer by the number of items of data.

Median The second type of average. It is the middle value in a set of data which are in order of size from highest to lowest or lowest to highest.

Metric The system of measurements usually used in Europe and the most commonly used system in science.

Mode The value that occurs the most often in a set of data.

Negative number A number with a value of less than 0.

Net The pattern made by a three-dimensional shape when it is cut into its construction template and then laid flat.

Number, cube The sequence of cube numbers is 1, 8, 27, 64, 125, etc. It is made up from $1 \times 1 \times 1$, $2 \times 2 \times 2$, $3 \times 3 \times 3$ and so on.

Number, prime A number with two and only two factors. The factors are the number itself and 1.

Number, square The sequence of square numbers is 1, 4, 9, 16, 25, 36, etc. It is made up from 1×1, 2×2, 3×3 and so on.

Numerator The upper part of a fraction.

Obtuse Refers to any angle greater than 90° but less than 180°.

P

Parallel lines Lines that are equidistant along the whole of their length, in other words they are a constant distance apart along the whole of their length.

Perimeter The total distance around the boundary of a shape.

Perpendicular lines Lines that meet at right angles.

Pie chart A chart in the shape of a circle, where the size of the sector shows the frequency.

Polygon A many-sided shape.

Powers The power to which a number is raised, also called 'indices'.

Prism A solid with a uniform cross-section.

Probability The study of the chance of events occurring.

Pythagoras' rule (theorem) The statement of a relationship between the three sides of a triangle, which is 'the square of the hypotenuse of a right-angled triangle is equal to the sum of the squares of the other two sides'. Using algebra, it is written as $h^2 = a^2 + b^2$.

Q

Quadratic equation An equation where the highest power is 2.

Quadrilateral A plane four-sided shape.

R

Radius The distance from the centre of a circle to any point on the remaining part of the circumference. So the radius is half of the diameter of the same circle.

Ratio The relationship between one quantity and another.

Rational number A number that can be written as a fraction.

Reflex angle Any angle greater than 180°.

Right angle Any angle that is equal to 90°.

S

Scalene triangle A triangle where all of the sides and all of the angles are of different sizes.

Sequences A set of numbers having a common property. A mathematician can work out what the numbers have in common and so predict further numbers in the sequence.

Standard deviation The square root of the variance. It is a measure of dispersion.

Standard form A way of writing very large or very small numbers, using powers of 10.

Surds Numbers often expressed as the square roots of a number.

T

Tangent A straight line that touches a circle at one point on its circumference.

V

Variance The mean of the deviations from the mean of a set of data.

VAT Value Added Tax.

Last-minute learner

Number

Types of numbers
- **Integers** are positive and negative whole numbers. **Rational numbers** include integers and fractions. Numbers such as $\sqrt{2}$, $\sqrt[3]{10}$ and π are irrational.
- **Multiples** of a number are in its multiplication table. **Common multiples** are multiples of two or more different numbers. Any group of numbers has a **lowest common multiple** (LCM).
- **Factors** of a number are other numbers that divide into it without leaving a remainder. A **prime** number only has two factors: 1 and the number itself, eg 2, 3, 5, 7, 11... A number that isn't prime is **composite**. Any number can be written as a product of **prime factors**.
- **Common factors** are factors of two or more numbers. Any group of numbers has a **highest common factor** (HCF).

Indices
- **Powers** are made by multiplying a number (the **base**) by itself repeatedly. The **index** tells you how many copies of the base to multiply. Any number to the first power is just the number (eg $10^1 = 10$). Any number to the zeroth power is 1 (eg $5^0 = 1$).
- **Roots** are the opposite or **inverse** of powers. The **square root** of 9 is written $\sqrt{9} = 3$. The **cube root** of 343 is written $\sqrt[3]{343} = 7$.
- **Index laws**: in algebra, $a^n \times a^m = a^{(n+m)}$, $a^n \div a^m = a^{(n-m)}$.
- A negative power is just the **reciprocal** of the positive power. $2^{-2} = \frac{1}{2^2} = \frac{1}{4}$, $2^{-3} = \frac{1}{2^3} = \frac{1}{8}$, etc.
- **Fractional** indices mean **roots**.
- Numbers in **standard index form** consist of a power of 10 multiplying the significant digits of the number.
  2 million $= 2 \times 1\,000\,000 = 2 \times 10^6$
  2 500 000 $= 2.5$ million $= 2.5 \times 10^6$
- Numbers less than 1 need a negative index, eg $0.002\,13 = 2.13 \times 10^{-3}$

Fractions
- You can only **add or subtract** fractions if they have the same denominator. To add or subtract fractions with different denominators, change to equivalent fractions with equal denominators.
- To **multiply** two fractions together, just multiply the top and bottom numbers separately. Convert mixed fractions to improper ones first. To divide two fractions, invert the second one (turn it upside down) and turn the $\div$ into a $\times$.
- To find $\frac{1}{n}$ of something, divide by n. To find other fractions, first work out $\frac{1}{n}$, then multiply by the numerator.

Proportion and ratio
- There are two main ways to work out a **percentage** of something: either divide the amount by 100 to find 1%, then multiply by the number of per cent; or convert the percentage to a decimal, then multiply the amount by this.
- There are two ways to calculate the result of a percentage **increase or decrease**: work out the amount of change and add/subtract it; or work out the new percentage required and calculate it.
- A **reverse change** is one where you know the amount after a percentage change and want to find the original amount.
- If y is **directly proportional** to x, this is written $y \propto x$. That means $y = kx$, where k is the **constant of proportionality**. Two proportional amounts plotted against each other on a **graph** give a straight line through the origin.
- Amounts that are in direct proportion are also in a constant **ratio**. Ratios can be equivalent to each other, just like fractions. So $10 : 4 = 20 : 8 = 100 : 40 = 5 : 2$ in lowest terms. Ratios can also be written in unitary form (containing a 1). $10 : 4 = 1 : 0.4. = 2.5 : 1$
- Sometimes you need to divide amounts in a certain ratio. Add up the numbers in the ratio to get the total number of 'shares', find the value of one 'share', then calculate the parts as required.

Data handling

Processing data
- The **mode** is the most common value. In the case of data in groups or classes, the group with the highest frequency is called the **modal group** or class.
- The **median** is the middle value in a set, when all the numbers are in order. If you have an even number of data, the median is halfway between the two in the middle.
- The **mean** is the most frequently used average. It is calculated by taking the sum of all the data items, then dividing by the number of items.
- **Range** is the difference between smallest and largest data.

Probability
- **Theoretical probability** is calculated by analysing a situation mathematically. The probability can be used to predict the expected frequency of the outcomes of a number of **trials**.
- **Experimental probability** is determined by analysing the results of a number of trials of the event.
- The **OR rule**: when two outcomes A and B of the same event are exclusive, $P(A \text{ or } B) = P(A) + P(B)$.
- The **AND rule**: When two events X and Y are independent, $P(X \text{ and } Y) = P(X) \times P(Y)$.

Shape, space and measures

Accuracy of measurements

- Suppose the length L of a piece of wire is 67 mm, to the nearest mm. Anything less than 66.5 mm would round down to 66 mm. Anything 67.5 mm and above would round up to 68 mm. So $66.5 \leqslant L < 67.5$.
  If L is given to the nearest 0.1 mm (1 dp) instead, then $66.95 \leqslant L < 67.05$.

Speed, distance and time

- Units of speed are metres per second (m/s), kilometres per hour (km/h), miles per hour (mph), etc.
- Use the 'd-s-t triangle'. Cover up the letter you want to work out: the triangle gives the formula.

Mensuration – length and distance

- In any right-angled triangle, the **hypotenuse** is the side opposite the right angle.

- **Pythagoras' rule (theorem)**: in any right-angled triangle, $h^2 = a^2 + b^2$. Use it to calculate the diagonal of a rectangle, or the distance between two points on a co-ordinate grid.
- The **circumference** of a circle of diameter d (radius r) is $C = \pi d = 2\pi r$. Note that $\pi \approx 3.142$.
- When a wheel turns once (makes one **revolution**), the distance moved by whatever it is attached to (eg a car or a bike) is the same as the circumference of the wheel.

Area

- Using l for length and w for width, the area A of a rectangle is given by $A = lw$
- Triangles, parallelograms and trapezia all share an important measurement: the **perpendicular height**. These are the area formulae:

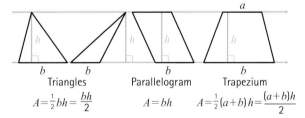

Triangles	Parallelogram	Trapezium
$A = \frac{1}{2}bh = \frac{bh}{2}$	$A = bh$	$A = \frac{1}{2}(a+b)h = \frac{(a+b)h}{2}$

- The area of the **circle** of radius r is $A = \pi r^2$

Surface area

- The surface area of a solid object is the combined area of all the faces on the outside. Curved surfaces on spheres, cones and cylinders form part of the surface area too.
- For a prism with cross-section of perimeter P and area A, the total surface area $S = 2A + Pl$. For a cylinder, $S = \pi rl + 2\pi rl = 2\pi r(r + l)$.

- Cones need an extra measurement, the slant height s. The curved surface is πrs, so the total surface area is $\pi r^2 + \pi rs = \pi r(r + s)$.
- The surface area of a sphere is $4\pi r^2$.

Volume

- There are four basic volume formulae.

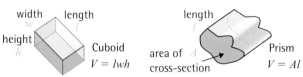

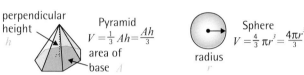

- For a cylinder, $V = \pi r^2 l$, and for a cone, $V = \frac{1}{3}\pi r^2 h = \frac{\pi r^2 h}{3}$.

  $1 \text{ cm}^2 = 1 \text{ ml}, 1 \text{ l} = 1000 \text{ cm}^2, 1000 \text{ l} = 1 \text{ m}^2$

Shapes and angles

- Whenever lines meet or **intersect**, the angles they make follow certain rules.

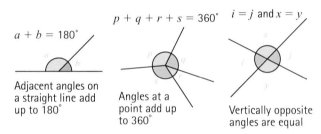

$a + b = 180°$ — Adjacent angles on a straight line add up to 180°

$p + q + r + s = 360°$ — Angles at a point add up to 360°

$i = j$ and $x = y$ — Vertically opposite angles are equal

- Three types of relationship between angles are produced when a line called a **transversal** crosses a pair of parallel lines.

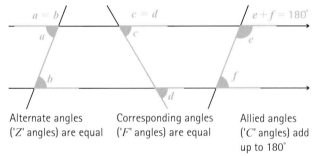

$a = b$ — Alternate angles ('Z' angles) are equal

$c = d$ — Corresponding angles ('F' angles) are equal

$e + f = 180°$ — Allied angles ('C' angles) add up to 180°

- The **exterior angles** of a **polygon** always add up to exactly 360°.
- Every type of polygon has its own **interior angle sum**. You can calculate it using any of these formulae: n is the number of sides and S is the angle sum.

  $S = (n - 2) \times 180°$ $S = (180n - 360)°$
  $S = (2n - 4)$ right angles

- Work out the interior angles for **regular** polygons in two ways: work out the angle sum, then divide by the number of sides; or divide 360° by the number of sides to find one exterior angle, then take this away from 180°.

Transformations

- Mathematical transformations start with an original point or shape (the **object**) and transform it (into the **image**).
- A **translation** is a 'sliding' movement, described by a **column vector**, eg $\begin{pmatrix} 5 \\ -4 \end{pmatrix}$.
- In a **rotation**, specify an angle and a fixed point called the **centre of rotation**. Given a rotation, you can usually find the centre by trial and error, using a piece of tracing paper.
- When an object is **reflected**, the object and image make a symmetrical pattern. Reflection in any line is possible, but the most likely ones you will be asked to use are these:
  - horizontal lines ($y = a$ for some value of a)
  - vertical lines ($x = b$ for some value of b)
  - lines parallel to $y = x$ ($y = x + a$ for some value of a)
  - lines parallel to $y = -x$ ($y = a - x$ for some value of a).

Enlargement

- To describe an enlargement you need to give a **scale factor** and a **centre of enlargement**. The scale factor affects the **size** of the image. The centre of enlargement affects the **position** of the image.

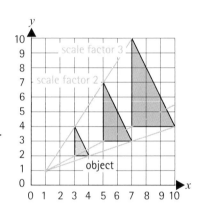

- To find the centre of enlargement, draw lines through corresponding points on the object and image. These all intersect at the centre of enlargement. To find the scale factor, divide the length of a line on the image by the corresponding line on the object.
- The scale factor of a model, map, or scale drawing is usually expressed as a ratio. A 1:40 scale model of a boat is $\frac{1}{40}$ of the actual size of the boat. A diagram of a circuit on a scale of 25:1 is 25 times larger than the real thing.

Congruent and similar shapes

- Two shapes that are identical are **congruent**.
- If the following features of two triangles match, the triangles are congruent: 3 sides (SSS); 2 sides and the included angle (SAS); 2 angles and a side (AAS); in a right-angled triangle, the hypotenuse and one other side (RHS).
- Shapes that are the same apart from their size are **similar**. Similar shapes are **enlargements** of each other. Two triangles are similar if they have identical angles. Their sides are automatically in the same **ratio**.

Loci

- A set of positions generated by a rule is called a **locus**. The four major types are as follows:

A fixed distance from a fixed point: a circle.

A fixed distance from a straight line: two parallel straight lines.

Equidistant from two fixed points: the perpendicular bisector of the points.

Equidistant from two straight lines: the bisectors of the angles between the lines.

- Often you need to combine information from two or more loci to solve a problem. Sometimes this will lead to a region or area, sometimes to a line segment, sometimes to one or more points.

Trigonometry

- In a right-angled triangle, the sides are given temporary 'names' according to where they are in relation to a chosen angle x.

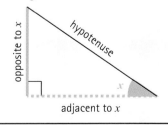

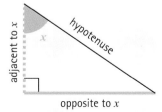

- In similar triangles, the three sides are always in the same ratio. These **trigonometric ratios** ('trig' ratios) have names.
- The **sine** of an angle is $\frac{\text{opposite side}}{\text{hypotenuse}} = \sin x$

  The **cosine** of an angle is $\frac{\text{adjacent side}}{\text{hypotenuse}} = \cos x$

  The **tangent** of an angle is $\frac{\text{opposite side}}{\text{adjacent side}} = \tan x$

- To find an angle in a right-angled triangle with known sides, calculate the trig ratio, then use the **inverse trig function** ($\sin^{-1}$, etc) on your calculator.

Algebra

Formulae and expressions

- **Substitution** is replacing letters in a formula, equation or expression by numbers (their **values**). Be careful to evaluate parts of the formula in the correct order.
- **Expressions** in algebra are made up of a number of **terms** added or subtracted together. Each term is made up of letters and numbers multiplied or divided together. Combine **like terms** to simplify an expression.
- A **formula** usually has its **subject** on the left-hand side of the equals sign and an expression on the right-hand side. Any letter in a formula can become the subject by rearranging it. As long as you do the same thing to both sides of your formula, it is still true.

Multiplying and dividing terms

- When **multiplying two terms** together, multiply the numbers first, then multiply the letters in turn, using the index rules.
- When **dividing terms**, write the question in fraction style if it is not already written that way and cancel the numbers as if you were cancelling a fraction to lowest terms, then divide the letters in turn.

Expanding brackets

- When a number or letter multiplies a bracket, **everything** inside the bracket is multiplied. Removing the brackets is called **expansion**.

Factorisation

- **Factorising** is the opposite of expansion. To factorise, look for **common factors** between the terms.
- This process is called **extracting factors**. Sometimes you need to do this in more than one step.
- **Quadratic** expressions can sometimes be factorised into two brackets. First write down a list of the numbers that could be part of the x^2 term. Write down a list of the numbers that could be part of the number term. Test combinations of these numbers to see if you can match the x term in the expression you want to factorise.

Basic equations

- The letter in an **equation** stands for a definite unknown number you have to find.
- To solve an equation:
  - think what you would have to do if you were substituting a number into the equation
  - to find the answer, do the inverse operations in the opposite order.

Trial and improvement

- Sometimes you can't find an exact solution to an equation but can find a reasonable **approximation** using trial and improvement. You use the results of a 'guess' to make better guesses.

Simultaneous equations

- Simultaneous equations are pairs of equations with two unknown letters that are both true at the same time. The technique of **elimination** involves adding or subtracting the equations so that one of the letters disappears (is eliminated). Sometimes, you have to multiply one or both of the equations. This is to match numbers in order to add or subtract and eliminate.
- Each equation in a simultaneous pair has its own **graph**. The x and y co-ordinates of the point where the graphs **intersect** gives the solution.

Inequalities

- Ranges of numbers are described using inequalities. You can illustrate an inequality on a number line.
- There are four inequality symbols:

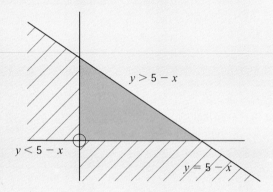

$>$ greater than $\geqslant$ greater than or equal to
$<$ less than $\leqslant$ less than or equal to
'All the numbers that are 3 or less' is described by the inequality $x \leqslant 3$ (or $3 \geqslant x$).

- Sometimes inequalities can be combined. Suppose that $x < 2$ and $x \geqslant -3$. This makes a **range inequality**: $-3 \leqslant x < 2$.
- A line (eg $y = 5 - x$) divides a co-ordinate grid into two **regions**. The region above the line is $y > 5 - x$ (see diagram) and the one below is $y < 5 - x$. The line can be included in the region by using $\leqslant$ or $\geqslant$.

Sequences

- Sequences are made up of a succession of **terms**. Each term has a **position** in the sequence: 1st, 2nd, etc. A **linear** sequence is one where the difference between terms is always the same number, such as 2, 5, 8, 11, 14, ... Using n to stand for the position in the sequence and u_n to stand for the term, this sequence has the formula $u_n = 3n - 1$.
- **Quadratic** sequences have formulae of the form $u_n = an^2 + bn + c$. To analyse quadratic sequences, you need to look at the **second** difference row.